Endorsements

In *Aligned for Conquest,* Clay Nash powerfully asserts that the true test of a properly aligned structure is a devastating storm, just as a ministry's resilience is revealed through attacks from the enemy. Clay's own journey reflects this truth, showcasing the longevity of his ministry and his ability to communicate timeless truths in relevant ways. This book serves as a crucial blueprint for believers, emphasizing that when we align ourselves with God and one another, we create a self-sustaining framework far stronger than our individual parts. *Aligned for Conquest* is essential for anyone seeking rapid Kingdom advancement.

Bishop Steve McCuin

******

Years ago, I asked the Lord why His people remained "stuck" in their relationship with Him. In response He gave me a Kingdom protocol that even Jesus followed. The first step in this protocol is ALIGNMENT. Everything in our life is the product of who and what we are aligned with. Alignment established the parameters of authority. Apostle Clay Nash in his book *Aligned for Conquest* offers us the most practical and insightful revelation about alignment that I've ever read! This book is an absolute must read for those who desire to be the Ekklesia on earth today!!!

Dr. Dwain Miller
Senior Pastor
The Edge Church Cabot, AR

******

Alignment that brings success/fulfillment always starts with God. Then we must align with everything God aligns with which He clearly sets

Endorsements

forth in His Word. Clay Nash has identified the key issues around alignment for this season that we have entered. God has great victory ahead of us, but we must first align with God and secondly those ordained by Him. Read this book, discover both what alignment means and the power of alignment. Then position yourself in alignment. The best is yet ahead!

Barbara J Yoder, Author
Founding and Overseeing Apostle
Shekinah Christian Church

******

Several years ago, the Lord began to speak a very firm and strong word to me. "I'm about ready to change the dynamic of My church. I'm about ready to show you what My church was truly designed to be." Over these last years, He has shown me time and time again that which was built by man and that which He desires to build as His ekklesia. This book by Clay demonstrates much of that restructuring and realignment. The Lord spoke to me clearly about the past season, structured by religion, that is about to end. It will no longer be about platform ministries but a grassroots movement that will arise. It will no longer be about a top-down structure of "covering" and overloading. An army, fashioned by God, representing millions upon millions of dedicated, Spirit-filled saints, will bring forth God's Kingdom and His will on earth as it is in heaven. He revealed to me two key illustrations of this transformation. The first, as Clay has mentioned, concerned a fishing net. As I picked up a fishing net that had been given me, He asked me, "Tom, which knot is yours?" I questioned His reasoning, but I reached out and touched one of them. And He said, "that's yours." He then asked me which is the most important knot. And I said, "You know Lord," and He said, "the one you just touched. If you are not properly aligned with all of the other knots of this net, then we can't accomplish what needs to be done for My Kingdom. You are going to have to be properly aligned." And then, on another day He asked me if I had considered the blade of grass. He went on to show me that if there's going to be a grassroots movement, then there must be the engagement, activation and alignment of every blade of grass. A great net has been formed called the ekklesia. A marvelous field, formed by a multitude of blades of grass, is laid out across the nation. God has aligned us. *Katartizō* is the word of the day, and Clay in his book, *Aligned for Conquest*, powerfully demonstrates this truth. It is the move of God which will bring about the ekklesia's conquest over all the forces of evil. To God be the glory. His Kingdom and will be done.

Dr. Tom Schlueter
Prince of Peace House of Prayer – Pastor
Texas Apostolic Prayer Network – Coordinator

******

Reading in the first chapter, Clay made this statement, "Alignment happens when we share life together." I understand that statement thoroughly. My wife and I have shared our lives together with Clay and Susan now for over 42 yrs. Clay and Susan helped move us to Dallas, TX New Year's Eve 1986, where we would attend Christ for the Nations Bible Institute. In Jan 1990, we joined them in starting Christ the King Church in Dyersburg, TN. We've been on numerous mission work trips together, broken bread together, broken down together, and broken up fallow ground together. By the Word of the Lord from Clay in 2013 on the UCA campus in Conway, AR., the ministry we now pastor and lead, CityGate Heber Springs, was initiated. We have lived, laughed, loved, and languished together. We taught his children in children's church and he has baptized ours in his swimming pool. I have the utmost respect and honor for Clay Nash. He is a man of integrity, honesty, purpose, and resolve. The truths he presents in this manuscript are ones he lives out every day. It is an honor to call him my friend, and a pleasure to recommend this book to you.

Dwayne Hardwick
CityGate, Heber Springs

******

Endorsements

Clay's book, *Aligned for Conquest*, reflects the God-given principles he lives by—principles that have profoundly impacted my life as I've gotten to know him. From the moment we met, Clay showed me the importance of genuine alignment and vulnerability as brothers in Christ. He took a chance on me, accepting an invitation to preach at a tent revival before we'd ever met in person. His openness and authenticity instantly struck a chord, and what began as a chance meeting has grown into a cherished, covenant friendship. Clay has shown me firsthand the power of aligning with others and stepping beyond a "me-focused" faith. He has taught me that we can't fully become who Christ intends us to be without connecting with one another through deep, covenant relationships. He renewed my faith in the proper role of authority and helped me heal from past abuse by spiritual leaders. His friendship and guidance have enriched my life in countless ways. I am deeply grateful for Clay and the wisdom he shares in this book. *Aligned for Conquest* isn't just a book—it's an invitation to experience transformation and growth in your Christian walk. Read it, and you'll find yourself yearning for a deeper, more authentic intimacy with God and others.

Brandon Burden
President & Founder Daniel Nation, PBC

******

This excellent book by my friend and colleague is a must read! I believe as you read, you will be informed, inspired, and strengthened in your life, and matured in your Kingdom assignments!

Clay has skillfully blended the following elements in order to impart to us an equipping manual that pulsates with life and Spirit-led strategies. The elements are:

(1) Biblical
(2) Theological
(3) Autobiographical
(4) Missional

(5) Historical
(6) Practical
(7) Testimonial

You won't find a better understanding and explanation of our alignments in the Kingdom of God than this volume!

This book doesn't have a hint of religion in it. But it does have a heavy dose of reality in it. The English alphabet begins with the letter "A". The Kingdom of God begins with the revelation of the Alignment in the third heaven between Father God and His Son Who sits at His right hand. Their alignment is the foundation for our alignments as sons and daughters of The Father and as servants of our King Jesus. Clay is a five-star general in the Army of the Lord God. The anointing on him and his ministry will stir you about conquering the enemies of the Gospel in a new way. Use this book to teach and train fellow-soldiers in Christ.

Jim Hodges
Founder and President
Federation of Ministers and Churches International

******

It is my joy to recommend Clay's newest book, *Aligned for Conquest*. As one privileged to be aligned with Clay and other apostolic leaders, I can speak to the power and protection it brings individually and corporately. We are better together. The days of the Lone Ranger are over. Those who choose to go it alone are usually wounded warriors who have not been healed of their past traumas. The corporate revelation received through a team is exponential. One plus one is greater than two when it is accomplished together. God gets the glory and don't forget David's mighty men! They accomplished the impossible. They could not have done it alone. As you read this book, you will see the power of alignment and see the importance of stepping into your place in the army of the Lord. Each chapter brings greater understanding of the importance of coming together to accomplish

Endorsements

seemingly insurmountable tasks. We are better together. Read this book, find your tribe, and work together to accomplish assignments given by Holy Spirit.

Regina Shank
Global Transformation International

******

Well, Clay has done it again! In his new book, *Aligned for Conquest,* he has addressed a huge foundational need in the church. *Aligned for Conquest* not only addresses problems, but Clay also adds tested solutions. Don't we all wish we'd have known these truths when we started in ministry. Clay's Prophet anointing, and some Arkansas sass, speaks of alignment with integrity, and nothing will be functional until it is first relational. It is not just aligning; the issue is proper aligning, with mutual trust and honor. Ministry leaders and the church must have these safeguards. Thanks, Clay, with these nuggets we may be *Aligned for Conquest*!

Apostle Jerald Freeman
Ascension Church, Skiatook Oklahoma

******

Alignment for the assignment! Awesome read! Full of wisdom and insight into Kingdom dynamics. A clear roadmap into corporate authority that the Ekklesia must embrace. Clay clearly has years of experiential wisdom manifest in its pages. It should be kept as a how-to manual/reference book for all leadership in the kingdom for years to come.

Pastor R. D. Owens
Glory Barn Branson, MO

******

In *Aligned for Conquest*, my friend Clay Nash brings much needed understanding to the issue of biblical alignment. Knowing what something really looks like should be the priority of anyone hoping to find the thing they are looking for. With stories, testimonies, and descriptions of biblical alignment Clay makes recognizing this essential spiritual "growth hormone" less of the issue than whether or not we really want it. And in this humorous illustration he describes how serious it can be to procrastinate about developing alignment. "It's like the guy whose house was invaded by robbers, and he ran to the garage and began lifting weights. Too late, buddy." However, Clay warns us it won't be easy because, "Alignment is warfare." When the devil so viciously opposes something as he does biblical alignment in the Body of Christ, it should motivate us to do whatever it takes to "get it". The insights and experiences shared in this book define biblical alignment and its purpose in such a way that the reader can "get it".

Pastor David Hertel
Hope Fellowship

******

Now more than ever it is vitally important for believers to be rightly joined together in the troop God has assigned us to. We cannot accomplish what the Lord has destined us for on our own. I have been blessed beyond measure as I gain an understanding of what it means to be "rightly joined together" and learn to walk with the body of Christ. I have learned much of this from Clay Nash and as I tell him often "I love being part of our troop". You will never accomplish all that God has for you by yourself, this book will help you understand what proper alignment is and how to get there.

Mary Bentley
AR State Representative

******

Alignment is not about comfort, but about conquest. If anything, alignment is about discomfort (chiropractic) that brings integrity, definition, order, and stability to position us for conquest. No one has taught this better than our spiritual father, Clay Nash. The words on

Endorsements

these pages will challenge and disrupt your concept of alignment and bring integrity (framework) and language (definition) to biblical, relational alignment. This is done, in true Clay-fashion, not just through words spoken resulting in knowledge, but lived-experiences of his life, family, business, and ministry resulting in *revelation* and *wisdom*.

We have learned that you don't get aligned through simply living life, you actually get misaligned through living life (crisis, disappointments, transitions). Alignment is needed through relational covenant, prophetic leadership, and biblical-kingdom values. If God desires "fitly joined together," then the devil desires "misfit" and "disjointed." We have benefitted immeasurably in life, family, and ministry through our relational alignment with Clay and Susan. We encourage any person in ministry, but especially young leaders, to find the fathers and mothers in their lives, find biblical, prophetic, relational alignment… and then conquest will inevitably, and much more easily, come forth. Start with this text as a foundation for alignment in your life and ministry.

Matt & Natalie Coss
Worship Leaders, The CityGate Southaven
Southaven, MS /Memphis, TN

******

Aligned For Conquest is an in-depth and exciting presentation of how we work with God and the Body of Christ in the last days. In this book Clay Nash explains unity, oneness and alignment. I thought I was aligned with another organization for many years, but after reading this book, I see that I was in unity not alignment. When I met Clay Nash, I knew I needed what he had and chose to be in alignment with him. Our ministry began to take off and I saw my purpose for ministry. God bless you Clay for blessing the Body of Christ with this book!

Pastor Eddie W Thompson
Impact Church of Norman, OK

******

Aligned for Conquest

It is an honor to submit this endorsement for Apostle Clay Nash's newest book, *Aligned for Conquest*. In each page, I envision myself sitting in his living room as he pours wisdom, knowledge, and understanding into my spiritual heart. He has a unique gift that not only knows the Word and the Spirit of the Father, but also has the ability to convey how both operate in one's everyday life. He is a wise and gifted communicator.

Alignments are critical in the age in which we are living. Some are for a season; others are for a lifetime. But in each divine alignment there is something to be learned and gained as one progresses in the pursuit of oneness with the Father and one another.

In the pages that follow, you will learn what true alignment looks like, how Father designed it, how it is meant to operate, the benefits and blessings that it provides, and the responsibilities one shares with others in the process.

You will discover the difference between traditional spiritual covering and the synergy that is present in divinely appointed alignments.

You will gain a true understanding of honor, submission, integrity, safety, and strength that flow through genuine alignment relationships.

Ultimately you will learn the true meaning of the love of the Father for you and one another as you navigate spiritual life and mission through divine alignments. I am blessed to be aligned with Apostle Clay Nash and other amazing fathers and mothers of the faith. Each occupies the deep places of my heart and soul, and each adds value and strength to my spirit.

As you read through the pages of this amazing book, may you receive revelation that not only encourages you but also sets you on the pathway of pursuit. Divine alignments await you.

Larry Burden, Founder, Kingdom Life International Kingdom Life Apostolic Ministries

Aligned For Conquest

Clay Nash

Copyright

Aligned for Conquest

By Clay Nash

Copyright © 2024 by Clay Nash

All rights reserved. This book is protected by the copyright laws of the United States of America. This book may not be copied or reprinted for commercial gain or profit. The use of short quotations or occasional page copying for personal or group study is encouraged. Permission will be granted upon request from Clay Nash. Unless otherwise stated, all biblical quotations are taken from the New King James Version. All rights reserved. Any emphasis added to Scripture quotations is the author's own.

Scripture quotations marked NASB are taken from the New American Standard Bible, © 1960, 1962, 1963, 1968, 1971, 1972, 1973, 1975, 1977, 1995 by the Lockman Foundation. Used by permission.

Scripture quotations, unless otherwise indicated, are taken from the New King James Version, © 1982 by Thomas Nelson, Inc. Used by permission.

Scripture quotations marked TPT are taken from The Passion Translation, © 2022 BroadStreet® Publishing Group, LLC. All Rights Reserved. Used by permission.

Scripture quotations marked MSG are taken from The Message, © 1993, 1994, 1995, 1996, 2000, 2001, 2002 by NavPress. Used by permission.

Editing by Jim Bryson (JamesLBryson@gmail.com)

Graphics by David Munoz (davidmunoznvtn@gmail.com)

Contents

Foreword 1

1. At Its Core 7
2. Alignment 9
3. Katartizo – The Power of Alignment 21
4. Aligned in Life 29
5. New Alignments For New Assignments 43
6. The Church Aligned 57
7. The Power of Agreement 69
8. Unity and Oneness 81
9. Aligned Through Commissioning 97
10. Authority and Leadership 115
11. Faith, Favor and Providence 137
Conclusion 155

Dedication

I DEDICATE THIS BOOK TO ALL WHOM I HAVE FAILED. To those who were disappointed with my leadership style, who were challenged by our relational alignment, and who eventually went elsewhere seeking a Kingdom connection.

I am certainly aware that I disappointed you, I frustrated you, and as some have reported, you became wounded.

From the depths of my heart, I am sorry. I ask for your forgiveness.

As a man called and sent by God, I was not perfect then, nor am I perfect today. However, I am better today than I ever was, and I will be even better tomorrow. I thank you all for your part in that process—those able to stand with me, and those who could not.

When God said "all things work together for good to those who love God and are called according to Christ's purpose," He certainly meant all things—the good and the bad, the rough roads and the easy roads.

"Can two walk together unless they agree?" Sadly, they cannot, and many have chosen over the years to change course and move on.

To these, my Kingdom brothers and sisters, I say: We did not discover that road of agreement together, and we suffered from it. Still, I bless you, wherever you are in your walk today, and I pray you find alignment, worthy of your heart's desire, for all the conquests ahead.

Whether aligned in fellowship or following different paths, we are all united under God, indivisible, with liberty and justice for all.

May God richly bless you.

Clay Nash

Foreword

By Jane Hamon

I WAS DRIVING DOWN HIGHWAY 98, the four-lane highway that runs in front of our church and home. My hands were tight on the steering wheel. Earlier that day, I had hit a curb (no jokes about my driving skills!) and apparently knocked my wheels out of alignment. I was having a hard time keeping my car from pulling to the right. What should have been a pleasant drive home became a battle stay on the road. It was dangerous. I had to be careful not to slide off course into the other lane or even off the road completely.

When I got home, I reported this condition to my husband, who promptly arranged to have the wheels aligned.

Alignment is essential if we want to get where we are going without difficulties along our path. Alignment keeps us on course and surrounds us with protection.

By definition, the word *alignment* means:

To put two or more things into a straight line or to form a straight line; to be the same or similar; to agree with each other; to agree with or support another person, group, organization or view.[1]

In scripture, it comes from the Greek word *katartizo*, meaning:

To complete thoroughly, to repair, adjust, fit, frame, mend, to put in order, to equip, strengthen, to make one what he ought to be.[2]

Spiritually speaking, each of us must ask ourselves:

- With whom or what am I aligning my life?
- What am I consciously (or sub-consciously) coming into agreement with that is affecting my life?
- How am I being fitted or framed together with others whom I might be strengthened, equipped and set in order?
- Am I becoming what I was made to be?

If we are not intentional about how we align our lives with biblical principles, spiritual leaders and prophetic assignments, we will find ourselves constantly being pulled in wrong directions and even sliding off course on our spiritual journey.

We see a beautiful prophetic picture of alignment in Ezekiel 37, when God takes the prophet to view the valley of dry bones. Ezekiel sees bones scattered along the valley floor—a picture of a defeated army that the victor did not even allow to bury their dead. Yet God speaks to the prophet:

"Son of man, can these bones live?"

I love the prophet's answer.

"O Lord God, you know!"

In other words, "Lord, you must know something I don't, seeing as this situation is hopeless."

---

[1] (https://dictionary.cambridge.org/us/dictionary/english/align)
[2] (Strongs Concordance #2675, Thayers Greek English Lexicon of the New Testament, Baker Book House, Grand Rapids., MI, 1977, pg 336, #2675)

Foreword

God's answer to Ezekiel was succinct:

"Prophesy to these bones, and say to them, 'O dry bones, hear the word of the Lord!'"

The phrase "dry bones" in Hebrew comes from the convergence of three words: *shame, confusion* and *disappointment*. These are heart positions that can cause us to get out of alignment.

So, the prophet releases a prophetic word that brings an awakening, a shaking, and finally, alignment. The bones wake up and properly connect/align with one another, facilitating full restoration and life. The bones are then covered in muscle and flesh and filled with the breath of God, arising as an exceedingly great army.

None of this was possible without the prophetic voice of God and the resultant alignment. Prophesying to the dry bones brought apostolic alignment that produced refinement and facilitated assignment.

Agreement brings alignment and fulfills assignment.

This is the same process at work in the ekklesia today. God is dealing with personal and corporate issues causing misalignment that produces confinement— a limitation on our strength, ability and capacity. His prophetic words are being released, not just to give us a picture of our future lives and ministries, but to align our hearts with the purposes of God, with apostolic and prophetic leaders, and with one another. Only then will we arise as the exceedingly great army in which God has called us to function. Only then will we see God's kingdom come and His will be done on earth as it is in heaven. Only then will we see the answers to our prayers as Matthew 18:19 says: "Again I say to you, if two of you agree on earth about anything they ask, it will be done for them by my Father in heaven."

Agreement brings alignment and fulfills assignment.

This is why this book is so critical for the ekklesia at this time. The Body of Christ has been fractured by doctrines, ideologies and even sin. We have been like the valley of scattered, defeated dry bones. Yet Jesus called his ekklesia a force to be reckoned with, against which the very gates of hell would not prevail. We are living in the days when God is bringing revelation of that reality. We are aligning as the ekklesia.

We are not called just to be a family…
 …although we are a family.
We are not called just as a healing center…
 …although we believe God for healing.
We are not called just to win souls…
 …although this is central to our faith.
We are called to be the ekklesia, a legislative body, an army.
We are called to march in rank.
We are called to alignment.
We are called to accomplish the transformation of cities and nations and to demonstrate God's kingdom on the earth.

My friend Clay Nash has undertaken this project because he understands what is at stake in the church and on the earth. I have known him for years and have always admired his laser focus on accomplishing his God-given assignment. He has invested himself to mentor others on every level. When some "hit the curb" and become misaligned, he boldly calls them back into a place of alignment and maturity so they can accomplish their own destiny and assignment, lending their newly aligned strength to others in the Body.

Clay is like Ezekiel, prophesying alignment to the valley of dry bones so that God might have His spiritual army in the earth.

My challenge to you, as you read this incredible book, is to ask the Lord to open your eyes to any area that may be out of alignment in your life: your marriage, your family, your mindset, your relationships, your spiritual covering, your spiritual tribe, your ungodly beliefs or

Foreword

wrong biblical concepts. It's time each of us comes into full alignment with God's present truth and divine purpose, so we can arise as that exceedingly great army, the ekklesia, against which the gates of hell cannot prevail.

Jane Hamon, Apostle, Christian International

1
At Its Core

TAKE ANY MAGNIFICENT STRUCTURE—a house, a bridge, a building, maybe the Eiffel Tower or the Arch in St. Louis—and strip it to its elements. Behind the surface, you'll find alignment. A skeletal framework will be at the core, supporting its inherent weight and resisting all forces that come against it: wind, vibration, corrosion, guided missiles. The strength of a structure is found in the alignment of the elements.

Skyscrapers are built from the ground up by aligning steel members one to one another, creating a complex, self-sustaining framework far stronger than the sum of its individual parts. In fact, alignment is so critical that a deviation of an eighth of an inch at ground level can be catastrophic at the 32nd floor.

Take the human body, that biological marvel that leaps and runs, bringing muscle and sinew to bear against every obstacle. Beneath the skin is a skeletal system comprised of a vast array of bones in perfect alignment, a construct that bears an incredible amount of force during our lifetimes.

Aligned for Conquest

We are marvelous creatures. We endure forces arrayed against us, forces intent on our destruction, yet we stand like the structures we build, aligned part by part, each member a component of quality. Assembled less skillfully, these structures soon collapse; our buildings would fall; our bridges would fail; our cities would be reduced to rubble; our bodies would break down.

A skillful builder knows how to select the right materials and assemble the parts. He knows that strength is in alignment, and he is certain that this goes further than mere bones and steel.

God is that skillful builder, and he is constructing his Ekklesia on earth.

> *And I also say to you that you are Peter, and upon this rock I will build My church (Ekklesia); and the gates of Hades will not overpower it.*
>
> Matthew 16:18

2
Alignment

IT HAD BEEN A TOUGH NIGHT for the Galilean fishermen. They had labored under a starlit sky, casting their nets and receiving little for their efforts. Now, a little past dawn, they were ready to quit. Not far from shore, another fisherman was having far more success. So much so, in fact, that when the crowds pressed into him, hungry for his every word, he called out to the beleaguered fishermen, stepped into their barren boat, and had them cast off from shore just far enough to still be heard but not assailed.

When Jesus finished teaching, he sent the crowd away, then told the fishermen, "Put out into the deep water and let down your nets for a catch."

Simon was skeptical. "Master, we worked hard all night and caught nothing, but I will do as you say and let down the nets."

When they did, the nets filled with so many fish that they were in danger of tearing.

"Follow Me," said Jesus as the fishermen hauled the bounty to the shore—easily a year's worth of income. "And I will make you fishers of people."

They didn't need any more persuading. Simon and his brother, Andrew, dropped their nets and followed Jesus.

It wasn't long until Jesus approached two other fishermen: James and John, who were mending their nets.

"Follow me," he said.

And they did.

That morning, two nets were cast: one for fish, the other for souls. Neither net could break without great loss. Fortunately, the nets held; they had to. In the Greek, the word for "mend" used in the phrase "mending their nets" is the word *katartizō*. It means "aligned."

The nets used by the fishermen needed to be aligned: one strand tied with another, expertly measured and joined, smaller strands for the inside of the net, stronger strands bordering the outside of the net to cast and retrieve. Alone, each single strand would break under the strain of the harvest. Twisted together as one dense cord, they would be unusable—a solid rope a foot thick. But skillfully aligned—light enough to be agile, strong enough to bear the load—they would bring in the harvest of a lifetime. Jesus spent three years constructing his net, and it yielded the Kingdom of God on the earth and the salvation of mankind.

Alignment

Alignment in the Body of Christ means different things to different people: authority, anointing, financial support, even fidelity—these qualities and more are wrapped up in the term *alignment*. For many years, Christians referred to alignment as "covering." It was fashionable to ask: "Whose covering are you under?"

One guy replied: "I dunno. I sleep with a quilt. My wife made it."

Alignment

Too often, what we referred to as a *covering* was really a *smothering*. We ended up laboring under one person's vision, and this truncated our effectiveness, held us inside four walls, and caused us to second-guess everything God was saying to us. Of course, four walls are important—outdoor meetings are great until it rains or the rental company wants their tent back—but we cannot ignore what God is doing throughout the earth in a variety of shapes and formats, often without a visible organization or structure.

Alignment is not about hierarchy. It's not a top-down plan for the subjection of the world through a Christian-themed bureaucracy. Alignment is about each of us, in relationship with one another, finding the best within us and multiplying it through the power of agreement.

Twenty-five years ago, the Lord said to me, "It is no longer optional to recognize my voice." Today, it is no longer optional to be aligned. Alignment isn't something we merely talk about. It's not something we do when the truck pulls to the left. It's something we must build if we hope to establish the Kingdom of God on earth. There's strength in alignment. There is honor, safety, and truth. Indeed, God's power flows through alignment.

We have known for generations that God's blessing, without the necessary maturity to receive it, will destroy us. Alignment is that maturity.

Alignment in Scripture

Let's look at the word *alignment* in scripture. The concept comes from Ephesians 4:11-13, where Paul outlines the five-fold ministry gifts and their function in the Body of Christ.

> *And He gave some as apostles, some as prophets, some as evangelists, some as pastors and teachers, for the equipping of the saints for the work of ministry, for the building up of the body of Christ; until we all attain to the unity of the faith, and of the knowledge of the Son of God, to a mature man, to*

the measure of the stature which belongs to the fullness of Christ.

After listing each of the five gifts, Paul gives us their purpose: "for the equipping of the saints...." Notice, however, that the totality of the gifts came first. All five were given...and only then did he give us their single purpose.

The word *equipping* in Greek is *katartizō*, meaning "to realign, mend, or repair." Much like a trip to the chiropractor, when you have been realigned, you are being perfected; you are being matured. The Body of Christ is immature because it is out of alignment.

When something is aligned, it is "fitly joined together," as we are told in the venerable King James Version.

A couple of years ago, I put brand new tires on our motor coach that we use in ministry. I also had it aligned, and it handled so much better. When something's out of alignment, it's not as effective as it is aligned. If you ever had your body get out of alignment, you know what I'm talking about. A crack here and a pop there and you are ready to play defense for the Chicago Bears!

Within that definition of alignment, however, is the implicit principle of alignment with integrity. We must be intentional about alignment, but we must also be skillful. Alignment yields power, and power comes in two varieties: good and bad. Don't take my word for it. Consider what God did in Genesis when all the world was both evil and aligned.

Now the whole earth had one language and one speech. And they said, "Come, let us build ourselves a city, and a tower whose top is in the heavens; let us make a name for ourselves, lest we be scattered abroad over the face of the whole earth."

Now all the earth used the same language and the same words.

Alignment

And they said, "Come, let's build ourselves a city, and a tower whose top will reach into heaven, and let's make a name for ourselves; otherwise we will be scattered abroad over the face of all the earth."

Now the Lord came down to see the city and the tower which the men had built. And the Lord said, "Behold, they are one people, and they all have the same language. And this is what they have started to do, and now nothing which they plan to do will be impossible for them. Come, let Us go down and confuse their language, so that they will not understand one another's speech." So the Lord scattered them abroad from there over the face of all the earth; and they stopped building the city.

Genesis 11:1, 4-8

At first glance, one might wonder what was wrong with everyone on earth being empowered. *That's what it's all about, right? Fill the earth and subdue it?* Well…no. It's about righteousness. It's not about advancing; it's about *what we are* advancing.

Alignment with integrity gets us fitly joined together "for the building up of the body of Christ."

Alignment without integrity gets us the Tower of Babel.

Let's look at a few more scriptures that speak to alignment.

> *Sacrifice and offering You did not desire,*
> *But a body You have prepared for Me.*

Hebrews 10:5

The word *prepared* comes from the Greek: *katartízō*. It is the same word that is translated "alignment." So, this is saying that the Body of Christ is properly prepared when the people are properly placed in alignment. Do you know we're preparing a body for Christ? We are becoming fitly joined together. When things are fitly joined together, synergy is the result.

> *By faith we understand that the worlds were <u>framed</u> by the word of God, so that the things which are seen were not made of things which are visible.*
>
> Hebrews 11:3

"By faith we understand that the worlds were framed...." Again, we have the word *katartizō*, which is translated "framed." The world was framed by the Word of God, bringing it into manageable boundaries.

In Romans, we have an interesting take on "prepared." This is also a translation of *katartizō*.

> *What if God, wanting to show His wrath and to make His power known, endured with much longsuffering the vessels of wrath <u>prepared</u> for destruction.*
>
> Romans 9:22

> *They said to Him, "Do You hear what these children are saying?"*
>
> *And Jesus said to them, "Yes. Have you never read, 'From the mouths of infants and nursing babies <u>You have prepared praise</u> for Yourself'?"*
>
> Matthew 21:16

The phrase "you have prepared praise" uses *katartizō* as well. We see here that even praise should be aligned.

> *And they overcame him because of the blood of the Lamb and because of the word of their testimony, and they did not love their life even when faced with death.*
>
> Revelation 12:11

It's a popular scripture, but one that is frequently mistranslated. Most Bible translations say: "and the word of *their* testimony." But the word *of* is not there. The correct word is *in*, as: "the word *in* their testimony...."

Alignment

Have you ever heard public testimony when the speaker said all the wrong words but the power of God was present? That's the distinction of "the word *in* their testimony." We overcome by the Lamb and the word *within us*. Our words have to be aligned with the Kingdom of God and the Word of God.

Safety, Strength and Power

Alignment brings safety. It surrounds us with those in spiritual authority. It protects us from the malignancy in others as much as it protects us from ourselves—our mistakes, our inadequacies, our immaturity and our inexperience.

A few years ago, I went through a difficult season that culminated with removing the ordination of someone I cared about very much. During that time, I erred on the side of mercy as much as I could. Finally, those leaders to whom I am accountable approached me and said: "You're doing too much. You need to shut this situation down."

I honored that word, knowing that they stood with me and would support me regardless of how things turned out.

Paul understood this as he wrote to the Thessalonians:

As we keep praying most earnestly night and day that we may see your faces, and <u>may complete what is lacking</u> in your faith?

1 Thessalonians 3:10

From the phrase: "may complete what is lacking…," *katartizō* is translated as "complete."

We are told in Hebrews:

Now may the God of peace who brought up our Lord Jesus from the dead, that great Shepherd of the sheep, through the blood of the everlasting covenant, <u>make you complete</u> in every good work to do His will, working in you what is well *pleasing in His sight, through Jesus Christ, to whom be glory forever and ever. Amen.*

Hebrews 13:20-21

That word *complete* is *katartizō*. It's saying to "make you aligned in every good work." Have you noticed that a lot of people who claim to be Christians today are not aligned with the word of God?

But may the God of all grace, who called us to His eternal glory by Christ Jesus, after you have suffered a while, perfect, establish, strengthen, and settle you.

1 Peter 5:10

Here, *katartizō* is translated as "establish, strengthen, and settle you." It's about the body of Christ coming fitly joined together.

In Exodus 3:5, God appeared to Moses in a blazing bush and told him: "Do not come near here; remove your sandals from your feet, for the place on which you are standing is holy ground."

What I've come to discover, by breaking down every word, is that God wasn't saying the ground was holy. Rather, he was saying "You're a holy man, Moses. If you touch the ground, it must respond to you and become holy."

When we have proper alignment with God and the body of Christ, we move into a place of authority. We can speak to things like Jesus told Peter:

I will give you the keys of the kingdom of heaven; and whatever you bind on earth shall have been bound in heaven, and whatever you loose on earth shall have been loosed in heaven.

Matthew 16:19

The Lord is bringing the church into a place of maturity. The good things that we aspired to do when we were immature, we're now able to do as mature sons and daughters of God. We can speak to things and

Alignment

see results. We can move things greater than the sum of our individual parts.

Proverbs 18:1 says:

A man through his own desires, will isolate himself and seek wisdom, but then argue or quarrel with it when it comes.

Alignment starts with relationship. You must be aligned with people. The person who isolates himself through his own desires is the one who will reject truth when it comes. People isolate themselves for many reasons, but the work of Holy Spirit is to bring us into alignment for the work of the Kingdom of God.

We cannot do what God is calling us to do in this present age without alignment. The era of the stalwart individual raging against the winds of opposition is over. It's time to align. It's time to harness the power of working together. It's time to embrace synergy.

Synergy

We understand synergy to be the interaction or cooperation of two or more organizations, substances, or other agents to produce a combined effect greater than the sum of their separate effects.

Basically, when two or more elements (people, machines, organizations) work together, the output is greater than the sum of the parts. Two tractors working a field might pull 100 hp each, but together, they will pull over 300 hp. That's the power of synergy. That's what Paul means by "fitly joined together."

Synergy can be understood from Deuteronomy 32:30.

> *How could one chase a thousand,*
> *And two put ten thousand to flight,*
> *Unless their Rock had sold them,*
> *And the Lord had surrendered them?*
> *For their rock is not as our Rock,*
> *Even our enemies themselves being judges*

Notice the math here. The warrior count doubled: 1 to 2. But the body count increased by an order of magnitude: 1,000 to 10,000. Similarly, one man might lift 200 pounds, but two men aligned and working together can lift over 500 pounds. That's the power of synergy.

Synergy doesn't come merely because we increase personnel, however. I've had people work beside me who actually slowed me down! They didn't create synergy. I spent the whole time doing my job and theirs while cleaning up their mistakes!

I knew a young man, Tom, who wrote me a letter asking me to mentor him. His father had abandoned him as a baby. He was the only boy surrounded by sisters. He came to work with me one summer. We were building a deck on the second floor of our house. I worked on a ladder, and Tom's job was to hand me tools. Only he wasn't very good at it because he had never worked with someone on a building project.

About the middle of the second day, I finally sat him down over a couple mason jars of ice-cold sweet tea. We talked about life, dreams, decks, ladders and nails. I listened to his stories and he listened to mine. Finally, I said, "Tom, you are going to have to learn to anticipate. You need to watch what I'm doing on that ladder. You need to know when I'll need more nails, a hammer, a level or whatever. It's not enough for me to ask and you to run off to find it. You need to have it ready before I need it."

Well, Tom got the lesson. He watched me like a cat watches a mouse. He was amazing. No sooner than the words left my mouth, I had what I needed. Soon, I gave up talking altogether. (I know…remarkable for me, right?) We finished that deck in time for him to return home to start school.

About three years later, he wrote me and said, "I just got the biggest promotion of my life, and it is all because of what you taught me on that deck job—to anticipate my boss' needs and be ready before he asks."

Alignment

I was proud of him. Notice, however, how that lesson was imparted. I didn't just teach Tom. I didn't set up a whiteboard and line out a diagram of Deck Building 101. Instead, I brought him into alignment. I accepted him as a mentee and he accepted me as a mentor. We talked at a deep level. He listened to me and accepted my authority. Only when we were in proper relationship could the lesson be conveyed.

You might wonder what was in that sweet tea (besides a pound of sugar). *Relationship*...that's what was in it. Learning how to relate to one another as a team is vital for alignment.

Alignment is not mystical. It's not some spooky connection that only the seers and intercessors can appreciate. It's practical. It's rooted in real life. It's established in the day-to-day of everyday life. And it benefits us all.

3

Katartizo – The Power of Alignment

By Dutch Sheets

SUCCEEDING IN LIFE requires continually adjusting and aligning.

Adjust: "to change (something) so that it fits or conforms; to adapt; to put in good working order; to bring to a proper state or position."

Align: "to arrange in a straight line; to bring into a line or alignment; to bring into cooperation or agreement with a particular group, party, or cause; to fall or come into line; to join with others in a cause."

The two work hand in hand. Adjustment is the process by which we are aligned.

Some adjustments are not that important, like tweaking the brightness of a TV screen. In other situations, however, being properly aligned is the difference between winning or losing, peace or turmoil, sickness or health, life or death.

Throughout my life, I've been adjusted and aligned. In fact, I have been adjusted so much, I've had adjustments to my adjustments! (Today, I might finally be fully adjusted.)

Growing up, my dad adjusted my attitude with a belt, menacing looks, strong words, the loss of privileges, and monetary deprivation. But it brought me into alignment. ("Yessir!")

In aligning with my wife, Ceci, and my two daughters, I've learned the art of communication, the importance of remembering birthdays, the proper remote-control etiquette (I hate commercials), the number of shoes a woman needs to function in life, and the broad-ranging effects of hormones and the phases of the moon.

Dentists have aligned my teeth to last longer and adjusted my jaws to feel better. (They've also taken a bite out of my wallet.)

Chiropractors have adjusted my back and neck to bring them into alignment. One said I had a subluxation.

"Subluxation? So, it's a sub-part of a regular luxation?" I asked, trying to appear knowledgeable.

"This is serious, Dutch," said my doctor without smiling.

"Good serious or bad serious?"

"Bad."

"Can you take it out?"

"No. You don't extract subluxations. Where have you been, the dentist? But if you come in twice a week for the next year, I can adjust you into alignment."

Two years later, I still don't know what a subluxation is, but I'm adjusted. (So is my bank balance.)

A few years back, I got aligned with my insurance adjuster in Colorado. I always wondered why they called them "adjusters." Then the pipes over my garage burst and he adjusted my thinking. Now I know what the insurance company *won't* pay to fix my pipes, repair the sheetrock, or restore my car.

By explaining all the fine print—the clauses, exceptions, and deductions—I realized I had been paying for peace of mind, knowing the adjuster would be there in an instant to adjust my thinking regarding what the insurance company would not do. (I certainly felt adjusted.)

Recently, I aligned with a policeman who adjusted my thinking toward speed. I also aligned with a jeweler regarding the value of rocks. And I aligned with my barista about the meteoric rise of coffee prices.

As you can see, I'm well-adjusted, aligned, and properly positioned to succeed in life. Glory to God!

The Heavenly Adjuster

God adjusts and aligns us. He has adjusted me many times: my heart, thinking, theology, direction, relationships, even my hopes and dreams. He does so to position us for the future. We cannot receive that for which we are unprepared.

What if I told you there was one New Testament word that encompasses all of the above definitions and more? Well, there is. The word is *katartizo*.[3] It has many nuances, all related to the concepts of alignment, connection, and/or position.

Here are some of the ways this word is translated:

- to properly position
- to establish
- to adjust
- to complete

---

[3] James Strong, The New Strong's Exhaustive Concordance of the Bible (Nashville, TN: Thomas Nelson Publishers, 1990), ref. no. 2675.

- to set (as in a broken bone)
- to equip
- to train
- to fully instruct
- to arrange
- to align
- to prepare
- to mend or repair

As you can see, proper positioning, alignment, and connection—*katartizo*—accomplishes much. Let's highlight a few of these uses.

Mending or Repairing

The concept of repairing can be seen by the use of *katartizo* in describing the "mending" of fishing nets (Matthew 4:21) and "restoring" broken lives (Galatians 6:1).

The word is also used to describe the reconnection of a dislocated joint or broken bone. When I broke my arm as a young child, the doctor *katartizo'd* it. As you can see, this word means "healing or mending through reconnection or realignment."

Applying this to spiritual or relational connection, we can say that properly connecting to one another brings health and healing. There is a reason that relationships gone sour are called "broken" relationships.

Connecting the Ages

The use of *katartizo* as "arranging" in the above list is fascinating. In Hebrews 11:3, God uses this word to describe Himself "arranging" or "positioning" the ages of time. The verse reads "the *aiones*[4] were *katartizo-ed* by the words of God."

Many translations of Scripture make it sound as though this is speaking only of physical creation. A more literal and accurate rendering, however, is that the "eons" or "ages" of time *(aiones)* were

---

[4] Ibid., ref. no. 5437

"arranged" *(katartizo)* by the word of the Lord. This is what Isaiah 46:10 means when telling us God declares the end from the beginning. This verse is not restricted to the physical universe but also refers to time and space.

J.B. Phillips's New Testament states, "The whole scheme of time and space was created [*katartizo*] by God's command..."

Wuest's translation says, "The material universe and the God-appointed ages of time were equipped and fitted [*katartizo*] by God's word..."

Young's Literal Translation says, "By faith, we understand the ages to have been prepared [*katartizo*] by a saying of God..."

The Passion Translation uses the word "coordinated" to describe God *katartizo-ing* the ages. Yahweh created not only the physical world but decreed the flow of time—the aligning and proper connecting of the ages.

God knew that breaches would occur in this timeline; indeed, breaks that would hinder our connection with Him and with one another. History would have "subluxations," as my chiropractor would say, and would need to be realigned and healed. Whether on a corporate level (e.g. Adam's fall, wars, racial division) or on a more individual level (e.g. broken relationships, personal loss, failure), there are torn places in history that need realignment and healing—*katartizo*.

This healing on a corporate or national level is referred to in Isaiah 58:12 (NASB).

> *Those from among you will rebuild the ancient ruins;*
> *You will raise up the age-old foundations;*
> *And you will be called the repairer of the breach,*
> *The restorer of the streets in which to dwell.*

This is also what is being spoken of in 2 Chronicles 7:14 (NASB):

If My people who are called by My name humble themselves and pray and seek My face and turn from their wicked ways, then I will hear from heaven, will forgive their sin and will heal their land.

God heals history's dislocations. He *katartizo's* the ages, not only declaring their alignment but, when necessary, their healing. We have a part to play in this through our repentance, forgiveness, prayer, fasting, prophetic decrees, and other biblical actions, all of which are honored and effective because of the blood of Jesus Christ.

The church is now moving into another season of realignment, repairing, rebuilding, restoring, and healing—*katartizo*. We find ourselves in a season where we can stand in the gap and see the past sins of nations cleansed and healed. (see Ezekiel 22:30-31). Spiritually dislocated regions and nations will be realigned according to the decreed plans and purposes of God.

Preparing and Equipping

There is an extremely important concept found in *katartizo:* "to equip, train, and prepare." Ephesians 4:11-12 (NASB) states:

And He gave some as apostles, and some as prophets, and some as evangelists, and some as pastors and teachers, for the equipping [katartizo] of the saints for the work of service, to the building up of the body of Christ."

Luke 6:40 (NASB) tells us:

A pupil is not above his teacher, but everyone, after he has been fully trained [katartizo], will be like his teacher.

So…why would *katartizo*—a word meaning "align or connect"— also be translated as "equipped" or "trained"? Because teaching, as spoken of in these verses, "connects" us to information, thereby equipping, training, and preparing us for a task.

Further, when people sit under the same teaching, they naturally align one to another; they *katartizo*. In Ephesians 4:11, "equip" believers is accomplished by properly connecting and aligning them together.

In the chapter, Christ compares His spiritual body—the church—to a human body. He describes the importance of each member individually and as properly connected to the rest of the body. Only then can it fulfill its unique function. When an arm is in its proper place, it is "equipped" (*katartizo*) to fulfill its purpose. Arms are not equipped to carry us. Legs do that. When all members are in their proper positions, they serve the body well. The five ministry gifts of Ephesians 4 "equip" the saints by overseeing their positioning and alignment in the body of Christ.

Proper connection also "equips" us because it allows life to flow from one "member" to another. Only when joined can each body part receive the blood-borne nourishment it needs. When disconnected, the body part dies.

This is just as true for Christ's spiritual body as it is for our physical bodies. Only through proper alignment and connection can power and life flow. All of us—including leaders—must be properly aligned and connected one to another, enabling us to release the life of God to others.

4

Aligned in Life

A SIGNIFICANT PART OF ALIGNMENT is knowing our God-created purpose. Christians today are immature because they don't know who they are, what their role is, and to whom they should be attached. We are all parts of the Body of Christ, yet we have toes walking around looking for shoulders; elbows trying to be a second ear; ankles trying to control fingers. Dr. Frankenstein would be proud.

Through a singular lack of spiritual fathering, people have resorted to aligning themselves. I can't say I blame them. The adage: "nature abhors a vacuum" applies to spiritual matters as well as physical. People have inherent drives. *I want to be this. I want to acquire that.* Sadly, nobody is telling them that the knee-bone's connected to the shin-bone. Immature believers attach and detach as they see fit. While I understand their predicament, the fact is, this renders them grossly ineffective for the work of the Kingdom of God.

Alignment flows naturally from spiritual fathering. When we understand what it is to be a son—a mature believer, male or female, seasoned and trustworthy—we realize the strength and obligation to be aligned with spiritual fathers. When we understand what we are in the body, our alignment becomes a matter of course. If I know I'm an ear, I will no longer resist my God-assigned placement on the side of the face. When we discover and accept what God created us for, we move beyond our insecurities, doubts, false pretense and posturing. We come into a place of peace.

Pop-Christianity focuses on signs that say Jesus is coming back at any moment. But he's not coming back at any moment. He's coming back at the *right* moment, and that moment is not now, because the Body is not ready for him. We are not aligned one to another. Too many kneecaps trying to be noses. Too many elbows ending up… (ah, never mind).

> *Having abolished in His flesh the enmity, that is, the law of commandments contained in ordinances, so as to create in Himself <u>one new man</u> from the two, thus making peace.*
> Ephesians 2:15 (NKJV)

God wants us to come into alignment so he can reign as the head. The One New Man wants to rise up. Yet it can only do so when it is fully aligned. When it does rise, it's not going to look like the Jews or Gentiles; it's not going to be male or female; it's not even going to look like Western or Arab. When the body of Christ comes together, it will look like Jesus. All of us…looking like all of Jesus.

Alignment with Spiritual Authority

> *And he [a leader] must have a good reputation with those outside the church, so that he will not fall into disgrace and the snare of the devil.*
> 1 Timothy 3:7

Alignment involves sharing your spirit with another, giving honor to those who are more esteemed than you, and being honored by those who esteem you as a spiritual leader. Certainly, all believers are sons and daughters of God; we are part of God's children. Yet spiritual authority is a process, and our reputation is built on something more than family affiliation. Alignment is about recognition of those with greater spiritual authority and experience; those possessed of qualities that we need to fulfill our assignments.

> *If you think you are a leader and nobody's following you, you're just out for a walk.*

Alignment is not about building a hierarchy. There is no organization of man that can do what God intends to do on earth. Still, the fact is that as we mature, there will be some with more authority in certain areas and less authority in other areas.

Naturally, we all gravitate toward relational leadership. It is a force that draws us. If you think you are a leader and nobody's following you, you're just out for a walk. There will always be those who want to follow leaders, just as there are those who want to be leaders. In truth, all of us follow leaders, and all of us are leaders in our own right. We align with certain leaders even as other people align with us.

The key to aligning with authentic leadership is understanding a person's reputation. The reputation of a leader comes from qualities like sustained relationships, financial solvency, moral purity, and effectiveness in building the Kingdom of God.

We find a good leader by asking:

- What have you accomplished?
- What's gone well? What's not so well?
- What have you learned?
- How's your personal life?

We find a good leader by examining things like:

- Have they backslidden every year for twenty years?
- Are their assets tied up in bankruptcy court?
- Are they being sued by their last three churches?
- Have their children burned them in effigy on live TV?

Then we can reasonably conclude that theirs is not a good reputation.

Our reputation is our backstory; that which follows us. If we are going to be aligned with others, we have to build a righteous history. It's all a matter of being known. Who knows us? What are we known for? This goes beyond the natural. (Everything goes beyond the natural; the natural and the spiritual are interwoven.) Even demons know to gauge a person's authority. When the seven sons of Sceva, a Jewish chief priest, tried to deliver a demon-possessed man like they saw the Apostle Paul do, the evil spirit met them with a challenge.

> *Jesus I <u>know</u>, and Paul I <u>know</u>; but who are you?*
>
> Acts 19:15

The words *know* in this scripture are actually two different words. The text should be translated: "Jesus I know, and Paul I am *getting* to know."

Put another way: "How much authority are y'all packing?" (Assuming the evil spirit was from the South.) In the case of these would-be deliverance ministers, their authority was not enough to effect the spiritual cleansing they desired. In fact, it didn't go well at all. They were fortunately to escape the encounter alive.

> *Then the man in whom the evil spirit was leaped on them, overpowered them, and prevailed against them, so that they fled out of that house naked and wounded.*
>
> Acts 19:16

We can't come fitly joined together until we allow someone with greater authority to help us find our place.

Proverbs 18:16 lays it out well:

> *A person's gift makes room for him*
> *And brings him before great people.*

Gifts bring us to great people, to those in authority, to leaders who can set a gifted person into proper alignment. You can be the best tailbone in the world, but if you keep trying to be the head, well…you get the picture.

When we embrace our place in the body according to God's original intent, we move with the flow of God's breath rather than on the momentum of our gifting alone. Giftings are great, and we all have them. They are important, but they are merely a starting place. Alignment with leaders sets us in place to fulfill our callings.

Paul describes this process when writing to the Galatians.

Then after three years I went up to Jerusalem to become acquainted with Cephas [Peter], and <u>stayed with him</u> fifteen days.

Galatians 1:18

The phrase "stayed with him" is translated "become acquainted with." It comes from the Greek: *historia*. It is where we get our word *history*. It is the only place in the New Testament that word is used. Paul was saying: "I went to Jerusalem to become acquainted with Peter; to get to know his history."

Paul made a similar statement when writing to the Corinthians.

For now we see in a mirror dimly, but then face to face; now I know in part, but then <u>I will know fully, just as I also have been fully known.</u>

1 Corinthians 13:12

Notice the phrase: "I will know fully just as I also have been fully known." It is impossible to know someone without revealing ourselves to them. Knowing is a two-way street. If I'm hiding from you, I will never get to know you; in fact, I can't really see you. I only see the reflection of my own ego. In the context of Paul's visit, he wanted to present himself to the Apostles. He was seeking alignment with them. He needed them, and they needed him.

> *It is impossible to know someone without revealing ourselves to them.*

When we align with others, it is more than "stand to be examined." Alignment happens when we share life together. When Paul went to Jerusalem, he did not just grab Peter by the robe and demand: "Hey! Let's align!" No, they spent many days together. They ate and drank, talked and prayed. They probably worshiped together. For all I know, they hunted together on Peter's land and shared communion in his deer stand.

Peter checked out Paul because he heard that some crazy man who used to kill Christians was now their greatest advocate.

Who are you?
What are you about?
What's real about you?
Where are your struggles?
Are the things I've heard about you true?

Peter wanted to know how Paul operated in the Kingdom of God before he aligned with him.

Likewise, Paul checked Peter out because he wanted to determine his authenticity.

Do you miss fishing?
Was the net really ready to break?
How'd it feel to deny Jesus three times and have him stare at you?

For alignment to be effective, it must be based on intimacy, and that comes through real life. You can pray with another person, worship and minister together, even read their books, but slide under the chassis of an aging Peterbilt and start busting knuckles together, and you'll find out what god they really call upon.

Alignment is not about gaining prestige. It's about intimacy, spending time together, revealing yourself, becoming vulnerable.

Alignment is relationship. I meet people all the time who try to boost their reputation by claiming they're in alignment with some important leader.

"That's great," I say. "Do you have their personal phone number?"

"Well, no."

"Have you been to their house? Shared a meal? Bounced their kids on your knee?"

"Come on, Clay. Their kids are grown."

"OK, fine. You donated a thousand dollars and they sent you an autograph postcard, and now it's on your refrigerator. But you're not really in alignment, are you?"

"Well…I guess not."

NEI Affiliation

Many churches are aligned with NEI (Network of Ekklesia International). Yet NEI is an endorsement of reputation, not a source of reputation. People often ask: "Aren't you part of NEI? Man, I have googled everything and I can't find NEI anywhere on the internet."

"That's because we do not have a website," I tell them. "We are not trying to recruit people into NEI. We are trying to build something that is relational first and functional second. We're not focused on increasing membership. We're focused on developing members."

See, you can align with an organization, a ministry—you can even align with a person's reputation—but it's not as life-giving as aligning with the person themselves. God is bringing the body of Christ together into alignment through true relationship.

Nothing will ever be functional until it is first relational.

That's worth tattooing on your arm.

Together in Life

Alignment occurs in unexpected ways.

In 1931, in Arkansas during the Great Depression, a black man, Robert, nearly dead from starvation, approached my grandfather. He rode an old mule that was nearly starved as well. And he said to my grandfather, "I will work for you for a week for food, and if I haven't worked enough that you can pay me, you don't owe me nothing."

Nothing will ever be functional until it is first relational.

My Grandfather hired Robert on the spot, and Robert became a part of our lives. He worked for the Nash family until 1978. Now, let me tell you the rest of the story.

In 1958, my dad had an explosion in the shop. He caught on fire, and while every other man in the shop ran for their lives, Robert dragged my dad out to safety. My dad laid nine months in Campbell's Clinic in Memphis, Tennessee. He eventually recovered.

Here's where this story ties to alignment and legitimacy. What if my grandfather had been a racist? What if he said, "You are a black man. I can't help you. Just go starve to death."

I'm sorry to say, that happened in those days, but my grandfather was not that way. Growing up, I worked many days with this man. I valued him. I probably loaned him five thousand dollars over my lifetime. He was always going to pay me on Saturday. I never saw it and I didn't care. I valued the man. In the providence of the Lord, in the law of the ultimate intangible, God brought Robert into my grandfather's life to save my dad's life. That was alignment; it had nothing to do with religion and everything to do with life. We were not Christians in those days, but we understood hard work and loyalty. And we never forgot a debt: good or bad.

When we understand the workings of God, we stop resisting alignment. We need to understand the mechanics of it. Many people feel they are aligned, but alignment can only take place between people's hearts.

Heart Chord

Alignment is a heart issue. Alignment is built up on a three-chord rope that is not easily broken.

> *Two are better than one,*
> *Because they have a good reward for their labor.*
> *For if they fall, one will lift up his companion.*
> *But woe to him who is alone when he falls,*
> *For he has no one to help him up.*
> *Again, if two lie down together, they will keep warm;*
> *But how can one be warm alone?*
> *Though one may be overpowered by another, two can withstand him.*
> *And a threefold cord is not quickly broken.*
>
> Ecclesiastes 4:9-12

1. Honor

The first cord is honor. We honor people: those who lead and those who serve. Alignment is built on honor. Honor is about submission, not just compliance.

Someone might ask me to do something that I consider trivial. I might do it out of compliance, but in my heart, I'm seething. "How dare they? I'm better than that!"

Submission is an attitude of the heart. Many people join or connect in one place for a while, then they join or connect somewhere else for a while. They can't seem to settle because they never come into true heart alignment.

Compliance will produce actions, and actions produce change. Yet change does not necessarily produce good fruit. The key is the spirit in which we act.

Submission, being a heart attitude, establishes a relational covenant by focusing on the spirit of the relationship: that which produces life. Through submission, I will do extraordinary things that I will not do through mere compliance. Obstacles that would stop a compliant attitude cannot withstand the determination of a heart submitted through alignment.

Through submission, I will do extraordinary things that I will not do through mere compliance.

When we examine the covenant of the New Testament, we realize it is better because it is relational. The old covenant was about man approaching God as a judge through the sacrifice of bulls and goats. The new covenant is about God approaching man as a father through the ultimate sacrifice of his first begotten Son. It is about being a son or daughter of God.

2. Integrity

The second chord is integrity. Many people define integrity as being right in what you say and do. However, that is more of a definition of character than integrity. The word *integrity* has to do with being fitly joined together.

> *integrity:* 1: firm adherence to a code of especially moral or artistic values: incorruptibility. 2: an unimpaired condition: soundness. 3: the quality or state of being complete or undivided: completeness.

The integrity of a building is how it is fitly joined together. Above a ceiling are trusses. They are supported by studs in the walls. These studs stand on sill plates attached to the foundation. The entire building stands, not just because of the quality of the materials, but also because of the quality of the construction—fitly joined together.

We are completed through our relationship with Father God, but like the root system of a tree, this extends to our relationships with each other. We must have integrity with the organizations to which we join ourselves. We must be aligned with integrity; we must be aligned through authentic relationship.

Many people want to align with me and NEI. I tell them, "Let's just walk together for a while. Because you might not like me after a year."

Hard to believe, I know, but sometimes people decide that they don't like me...for whatever reason. I guess that's fair. Sometimes I don't like them. If we walk together with integrity, we can truly understand one another. Separating from Clay Nash is not a sin. But aligning without integrity is sin that leads to worse sin. There is a strength that comes from integrity and a weakness that comes from a lack of integrity.

Susan's dad, a great man who is with the Lord now, built a horse barn with stalls. He was a horseman who trained walking horses and then got into spotted saddle horses. He built his barn, and when he finished building it, I said, "Mr. Riffey, they stick-built the trusses. They didn't buy them pre-made. Those trusses are not built correctly. If we ever have a big snow, which I know is not likely, but if we ever do, they are not going to hold together."

Well, my father-in-law was an honorable man and loyal to the builder. "Clay, that man built more barns than you ever have. I reckon it'll be just fine."

And that was the end of it. Like a good son-in-law, I shut my mouth and went about my business, being sure to tell Susan privately to never go in that barn during a storm.

About a year later, we had an eight-inch wet snow in Arkansas. Guess what? The barn fell in. It was sad. By then, the builder didn't want to come back and correct it. Now, had they built that barn with integrity—not good enough, but the best—it would have withstood the rare snowfall.

When leaders come to our church, they do not talk about how big we are, how rich the offering is, or how loudly we sing. Instead, they remark about the spiritual health of our people. We are healthy because we are fitly joined together. There is an integrity in our church.

- Where there is integrity, there is health.
- Where there is health, there is strength.
- Where there is strength there is hope.
- Where there is hope there is faith.

3. Relationship

The third chord is relationship. True alignment begins with relationship. You've got to spend time with each other, get to know one another on a practical level. As I said earlier, alignment is not restricted to the ethereal realm of the supernatural. It is formed in the practical aspects of everyday life. When Jesus gave the keys to the kingdom, he identified the inexorable blending between the natural and the spiritual.

> *Assuredly, I say to you, whatever you bind on earth [must already be] bound in heaven, and whatever you loose on earth [must already be] loosed in heaven.*
>
> Matthew 18:18

There is no dividing line, no gulf, no great chasm to be crossed to reach the spiritual. We are as close to it as we are to the physical. So start there.

Want to impact your city for the Kingdom of God?

- Open a soup kitchen in the worst part of town.
- Sponsor a day care for working mothers.
- Start an auto shop for the poor to get their cars fixed.

And watch the kingdom grow in the hearts of the recipients.

Susan and I have been married for over 50 years. Our communication has been a work in progress. We were married for several years before she set me down one day and shook me to my core.

"Clay, I do not like flowers that die in a few days. I prefer live flowers that I can plant in the ground."

Of course, that wasn't the way I heard it.

At the time, I was traveling all the time, and wherever I was, I had flowers delivered to her…just like it says on page 39 of *The Good Husband Manual*.

Well, I guess Susan didn't read the manual.

I finally broke down and asked for directions.

"Okay, honey. What do you like?"

"Diamonds."

"Diamonds? Huh…. Well, I'll have to work on that one. I don't know a good diamond delivery service, but I'm sure there's one somewhere. And while we're on the subject, I really don't like quiche."

I could see I had her there. It was quiche vs. diamonds. I tell you, sometimes you gotta get up pretty early to get the best of a Nash. Still, it was a start. We learned to communicate on a deeper level that day and we worked through some issues. Today, I love quiche, but I can't get her to cook it. And I'm still making payments on the Hope Diamond—the diamond I *hope* to get her someday.

Any alignment that is based on structure only and not a heart-to-heart relationship will have a short lifespan. Sometimes you want relationships to last. I recently had a long-term relationship disintegrate. It broke my heart. In my book *Relational Authority*, I wrote: "My greatest strength is I'm relational. My greatest weakness is that I am relational."

I had gotten several words about pulling back from this particular relationship, and I didn't. As a result, there was some contention in the separation. Had I pulled away as I was instructed a few years prior, it would not have gotten to the point it has. Sometimes, we are loyal to a fault.

The strength of alignment often comes down to a choice between gifting or loyalty. A leader can equip you with gifting if you have a loyal heart. He or she can take you to places you do not even know you wanted to go…if you have loyalty within you. If you are not loyal, you can't go anywhere. God is not going to let a leader pour into you on the level it takes to develop you. Structural alignment—alignment based on function—can produce fruit, but fails in the long run. Like my father-in-law's barn, it will stand for a while, but when the unexpected storm hits, it's going to fail.

5

New Alignments For New Assignments

By Jane Hamon

ONE NIGHT MY DAUGHTER-IN-LAW was putting her three sons, ages 3, 5, and 7, to bed. She was speaking to Aiden, the five-year-old:

"Now Aiden, I am getting ready to go put your brother to bed. But I need you to stay in your bed while I do. Do you understand?"

"Yes, Mommy," Aiden replied.

"Just to be clear, I don't want to come out and find you in the playroom playing with your toys. Stay in your bed. Do you understand?"

"Yes, Mommy," was Aiden's sincere reply.

However, when she came out of the other bedroom, she found Aiden in the playroom playing with his toys.

"Aiden, didn't I tell you to stay in your bed?" she said firmly.

"Yes, Mommy."

"Didn't I say I didn't want to come and find you playing with your toys?"

"Yes, Mommy."

"Then why did you get out of bed and come play with your toys?" she demanded.

"Well Mommy," said Aiden, pleading his case. "My head told me to stay in bed, but my heart told me to come play!"

Poor Aiden, he still got disciplined regardless of his reasoned and intelligent response. (As I recall, he lost toy privileges for week but was put on a waiting list for Columbia Law School.)

What was Aiden's problem?

It was simple. His head and his heart were not aligned. His misalignment caused disobedience, and his disobedience caused him great trouble.

In my almost 45 years of full-time ministry, I have watched the grief and suffering that misalignment causes in the lives of individuals, marriages, families, churches, businesses, and yes…even in our nation.

I have seen God-anointed, gifted individuals fall away from their walk with Christ and forfeit their personal destinies because they pursued money, position or personal glory. Internal wounding of the heart and soul, insecurity and dysfunction caused these individuals to be easily offended, discouraged or angered, causing them to walk away from all they once deemed important.

I have watched husbands and wives end up with broken relationships, broken families and divorce because they gradually became misaligned with one another, full of bitterness and unforgiveness, forgetting that when married couples come into agreement, their prayers are answered. (See I Peter 3:7)

I have seen churches destroyed because of a disconnect between the leadership and the people. When this happens multiple visions spring up, causing division and confusion. In the story of David and Absalom, we see how unity was destroyed, both because David could have led his family better and dealt with the Tamar situation more proactively, and also Absalom should have stayed in alignment with God's chosen leader regardless of his opinion or offense. His failure to do so eventually cost him not just his destiny but his life.

When we walk in alignment with God and others, the truths of God's Word are evident in the ways we choose to live our lives. Our thoughts, actions, choices and values are exemplified in each decision we make, how we treat one another and how we honor God. So many of the above cases could have had happy endings, had the individuals involved repented, changed their actions, and aligned with God's ways and God's leaders. It's not just a matter of *knowing* what is right, but *doing* what is right. True alignment will cause your heart and head to agree. (And maybe you'll get to keep your toys.)

Personal Alignment

So, you see, before we can discuss the benefits of spiritual alignment for kingdom assignments, which I would like to do later in this chapter, it is imperative we first embrace personal alignment and obedience with the Lord.

As you have already learned, alignment comes from the Greek word *katartizo*, meaning "perfecting, wholeness, completion, equipping," among other definitions. Part of the journey of discipleship for each Believer is studying the Word of God and submitting and aligning our lives to the principles and precepts found therein. If we spend our lives living out of our own desires, opinions, ideologies and mindsets, we will constantly find ourselves out of alignment with God's Word and His heart for us. When this happens, we will be like Aiden, with our heads telling us one thing and our hearts telling us another. This will breed chaos, dysfunction and disobedience in our choices and decisions. Indeed, it will lead to nothing but grief.

Many have not been raised in Christian homes nor taught to know God's truth. Some have experienced deep wounding from dysfunctional upbringings. Some have suffered from sexual, physical or verbal abuse that may warp their view of themselves, God and others. Some have survived horrific abandonment and rejection that twist perception and perspective. This leads to places of brokenness in our hearts and fragmentation in our souls that will constantly impair spiritual growth and maturity.

If we were to picture these areas of wounding as, for example, a broken leg, we would understand the importance of *katartizo*, (wholeness) in our lives. Other definitions of *katartizo* are "to repair, adjust, mend and restore." The first step in healing a broken leg is for the bones to be reset, re-aligned, so full healing can come.

My brother was a football player in high school and broke the bones in his hand more than once. Sadly, he did not recognize the damage done and did not see a doctor to reset the bones. He just sucked it up and went on. But later in his life, the function of his hand was impaired because the bones were misaligned when they healed. It took multiple surgeries to bring proper alignment so he could regain function.

So it is when we go through situations that wound our souls. We suck it up and just go on without going through the process of realignment: resetting our souls, forgiving others, resisting the devil and adjusting our mindsets. We heal, but in a way that lacks fullness. We lose function.

In every trial, we learn a lesson. Yet have we learned the right lesson? Or have we developed an ungodly belief that will misalign us with God and others, impairing relationships and limiting full function in spiritual service?

Alignment with God and biblical principles is the only way to experience the full blessings and benefits of salvation. Salvation is more than just escaping hell. It is experiencing the righteousness, peace and joy of living in God's kingdom here in the earthly realm. It means walking in freedom and wholeness, not just in eternity, but now, here in our lives on earth.

Therefore, we can define the process of discipleship in our walk with Christ as receiving the grace and truth from God's Word. This brings healing, freedom and alignment with God's heart and His ways, resulting in personal transformation in every area of our lives. John 8:32 tells us, "You shall know the truth and the truth shall make you free." Truth aligns us with God's purpose and power. This enables us to live in *katartizo*—fullness, completion and wholeness, fully repaired, mended and restored.

Aligning Our Mouths

It's not just a matter of getting our hearts and minds aligned, though it starts there, but it is also a matter of aligning how we speak. As a matter of fact, if you want to measure your level of faith and agreement with God's words, listen to what is coming out of your mouth. In Matthew 12:34, Jesus challenges the crowd by saying, "Out of the abundance of the heart, the mouth speaks." There is no such thing as saying, "Wow, where did that come from" or "I didn't mean what I said." If you said it, it came from somewhere in your heart.

A few years ago, my husband, Tom, and I were agreeing with one another and with God regarding some specific financial supply for a project. As we walked through an airport discussing some setbacks we had experienced, I said something that was completely negative and doubtful.

"Wow, we just aren't going to have enough money to finish this project! I don't know what we are going to do!"

Tom's head whipped around as he looked at me with his mouth gaping open as if to say, *I can't believe you just said that!* I actually popped myself in the mouth! Then I said, "I can't believe I said that."

Those words exposed the doubt in my mind and the unbelief in my heart.

Proverbs 18:21 says, "Death and life are in the power of the tongue." We often misquote this, saying "life and death." Yet death is listed first, I believe because it is our first inclination to speak death and doubt rather than life and faith. Proverbs 21:23 admonishes us, "Whoever guards his mouth and tongue keeps his soul from trouble."

Many times, Believers want to bind the devil and rebuke him for all our problems. In truth, we may need to bind ourselves and the words coming from our mouths. While I completely agree with breaking any curse the enemy may send against us, it is important to consider whether or not we are cursing ourselves by our words. Angels inhabit the atmosphere created over our lives when we speak words of faith, vision and joy. On the other hand, demonic forces may be empowered by our negative, fear-filled, angry, doubting words.

I have done a great deal of teaching on the power of making decrees over our lives, families, finances, churches, businesses, and even nations. Job 22:28 says, "You shall decree a thing and it shall be established for you, so light will shine on your way." Decrees are bold, faith-filled statements based on the Word of God, empowered by the Voice of God, which we speak out loud in agreement with the Holy Spirit. Speaking decrees is one way to bring alignment between your heart, mind and mouth.

When I have a need, or when I hear the Spirit of the Lord speak something to me, I partner with what He is saying by writing it down, finding corroborating scriptures and forming a statement I can speak out loud. Romans 10:17 says, "Faith comes by hearing and hearing by the Word of God." In other words, my faith has an opportunity to increase as I hear my own voice declare what God says. My own voice aligns my faith with the Word of God. As my heart and mind are built up in faith, it becomes less likely I will speak words of doubt and unbelief.

Psalms 81:10 in The Passion Translation declares, "Open your mouth with a mighty decree; I will fulfill it now, you'll see! The words that you speak, so shall it be!"

Aligning with God's Present Truth—Reformation

In 2 Peter, Peter knows his time on earth is growing short. He admonishes the church to live in a godly, righteous way and to remember all he has taught them to make their calling and election sure. Those who are aligning with the ways of God will receive the "great and precious promises" and become "partakers of His divine nature." Those who are misaligned are blind, which comes from a root word meaning "inflated with self-conceit and lifted up with pride" (Strongs 5187).

He then challenges them with these words: "Wherefore I will not be negligent to put you always in remembrance of these things, though you know them, and be established in the present truth" 2 Peter 1:12 (KJV).

What is "the present truth"? Present truth is the ability to function and operate in the fullest portion of revelation God has made available to us through His Word and His Spirit in the present age. It is important for each Believer to be established in God's present truth for the hour we are in. I am not talking about extra-biblical revelation, but rather to become full participants in God's restoration/reformation process. Alignment with all God has revealed of Himself over the past 500 years is imperative to our assignments for today.

Think about it! Just over five hundred years ago, there was no open revelation that was common to believers that salvation came by grace through faith, not by works. Yes, I realize Ephesians 2:8 was in the Bible all along, but it wasn't until Martin Luther made the radical statement, "The just shall live by faith" that those seeking salvation understood it wasn't through works or indulgences or confessing sins to a Catholic priest that would save them. It was through grace alone that they would be saved. This was the beginning of a five-hundred-year period of restoration of truth which the church has undergone.

During those five hundred years God emphasized truths that were always in the Word but lost during the thousand-year Dark Ages. With each restoration He expected His true followers to align with the "present truth" and embrace greater authority.

The next restored truth was the doctrine of baptism, not through sprinkling of infants, but by immersion of those who have been born again. For most of us, this is a common practice once one commits their lives to Christ, but hundreds of years ago, people were martyred for this belief.

Next was the revelation of holiness, the restored truth that we are not perpetually sinners but rather are made holy by the blood of the Lamb. The Holiness Movement brought the present truth that we should not live like the world, and that it is possible to live in a way that is pleasing to our Father as well as the understanding of the priesthood of the Believer. Each of us are kings and priests unto God. These beliefs ushered in the Second Great Awakening and massive revivals in the United States, England and even many nations. As we embrace the understanding of being kings and priests today, may it once again release revival fires throughout the earth.

Next was the Divine Healing Movement. Again, truths that were always in the Word of God, came into focus of restoration. Jesus died on the cross, not only to save our souls from hell and forgive our sin, but "by His stripes we were healed." Healing was also in the atonement. Though divine healing is a common belief for many of us today, it was considered radical just 150 years ago.

The 1900s saw the restoration of the ministry of the Holy Spirit with the Azuza Street revival in which the Holy Spirit was poured out

New Alignments For New Assignments

upon believers and they spoke in new tongues. It's estimated over two million people were saved as a result of this season of outpouring. Think about it! Just 120 years ago there was no open revelation about being filled with the Spirit, speaking in tongues or operating in the gifts of the Spirit.

In the last fifty years of the twentieth century, God began to restore the full function of the five-fold ministry to the church. "And He Himself gave some to be apostles, some prophets, some evangelists, and some pastors and teachers, for the equipping of the saints for the work of ministry, for the edifying of the body of Christ," (Ephesians 4:11-12 NKJV).

The word here for equipping is *katartismos*, a form of *katartizo*, meaning a complete furnishing, perfecting or equipping.

In the 1950s, God restored the function of the evangelist to the church. Many evangelists, such as Oral Roberts, Billy Graham and T.L. Osborn, traveled with tents, preaching salvation and often healing.

In the 1960s, God emphasized the ministry gift of the pastor. No longer was a pastor just a shepherd of a small church on the corner, but massive church growth, along with the Charismatic Renewal, saw large congregations spring up all over the world. Churches became less liturgical and more spirit-filled as pastors were empowered to raise up strong disciples.

The 1970s saw the resurgence of the ministry gift of the teacher. Before this time, pastors would preach a homily, with a message of encouragement to the faithful, generally lasting no more than thirty minutes. But teachers such as Kenneth Copeland, Kenneth Hagin, Derrick Prince, and so many others taught for hours, instructing believers to dig into and study the Word of God for themselves.

In the 1980s, we were blessed to be a part of the Prophetic Movement under the direction of Tom's father, Bishop Bill Hamon, who taught that there are modern-day apostles and prophets and that every saint can hear the voice of God. He wrote many books teaching on prophets, personal prophecy and the prophetic movement. He also wrote about God's restoration process of the Church so the Body of Christ would have an understanding of where we have come from and where we are going. He would not only prophesy over individuals by the hour, but also spent time training others to hear God's voice, activate the spiritual gifts which God gave them and see true New Testament prophets operating in the 20th and 21st century.

In the 1990s, we saw the restoration of the ministry gift of the apostle. Dr. Peter Wagner wrote many books on this subject as well as spearheaded the understanding that the word *apostle* means sent one. Each one is to be a "sent one" into the mountains of culture to bring an impact for the Kingdom of God.

> *The goal for the five-fold is not just to do the work, but to equip others to do the work.*

Why have I taken all this time to define each of these restorations? Because the goal of Ephesians 4:11-12 is not the restoration or function of the five-fold ministries, but rather the equipping (alignment) of the saints.

In the old paradigm:
- an evangelist wins souls
- a pastor counsels, nurtures and cares
- a teacher makes disciples
- a prophet prophesies
- an apostle plants churches and perhaps operates in signs and wonders.

In the new paradigm, the goal for the five-fold is not just to do the work, but to equip others to do the work. The goal is to have well-equipped saints. Each believer should be able to win souls, make disciples, counsel and care, prophesy and be a sent one. This is the picture of a *katartizo* army God is raising up today, one that is established in the present truth, empowered by the Holy Spirit and fully equipped for service.

Full Alignment for New Assignments

One of the present truth concepts we must align with is in regard to the identity of the church—God's Ekklesia. In Matthew 16, Jesus said, "I will build my church and the gates of hell will not prevail against it." From the beginning of the Catholic Church, we have commonly used the word *church* to denote a gathering place for Believers to worship and hear a message from the Word. Throughout the ages, churches created communities of believers who strengthened one another in their faith.

But it's only been over the past twenty-five years or so that God brought fresh revelation from the Word regarding this word *church*. We began to understand this word *ekklesia* was not derived from a spiritual word, but was rather a secular term describing those "called out" of the Greek community to form a legislative body that determined the laws and culture of the land. The ekklesia was the Greek Senate.

This term *ekklesia* was also used by the Romans as those "called out" from the military population to form a specialized task force with a mission to go into all the newly conquered Roman lands and make the territory look like Rome. The mandate was to establish laws that looked like Rome; build roads and buildings that looked like Rome; replicate Rome and its culture in this new territory.

This is the mission of the ekklesia: to make this earth look like heaven. We are called out to legislate and to bring transformation everywhere we go. We don't just "go to church." We "are the church" everywhere we go.

Tom and I have been local church leaders for over forty years. We love the church. We love times of worship and the Word together. We love our community. But it goes beyond that. We are an ekklesia. We are on a mission to this earth,

When we understand the governmental and military aspects of being an ekklesia, it brings our local mission into focus. It's not just about personal spiritual growth and fellowship, but we are being equipped—*katartizo-ed*—for a purpose: to bring transformation.

Accomplishing this will involve personal alignment of our own spiritual walk before God and others in the Body and also with our God-appointed leaders.

An army must align. It's not about individual soldiers just doing their own thing, but about hearing the voice of their leaders and the Voice of their Commander in Chief. Each soldier/believer understands their role and personal responsibility and faithfully takes their place to fulfill it.

We must hear the Voice of God individually for ourselves but also have the ability to submit to leaders who align many for the mission. As an individual, you may have a mission. But your mission becomes a "sub-mission" to a greater mission under anointed leadership. It is vital to the whole, where every part does its part to accomplish great things for God's Kingdom.

As an ekklesia, Tom and I have stewarded our territory. It was once the poorest county in Florida. We had the worst schools, corrupt law enforcement and non-existent growth and development. We were overrun with every kind of witchcraft and occult group.

To see things shift, we needed power-producing alignment. We began by aligning with God's heart to see our territory liberated from oppression. We also aligned with the Voice of God by hearing strategies from heaven to implement as we prayed. We further aligned by "marching in rank" by which I mean, each one brought their gift and what they heard from the Lord, but our apostolic/prophetic leadership team set the plan. Then it was time for deployment. We assigned team leaders to go to key places of influence in our community and initiate a spiritual strike.

New Alignments For New Assignments

This went on for months, if not years, with focused prayer, prophetic strategy and intercessory legislation. Over time it continued to be important to stay in alignment with the assignment until victory came. One by one, the strongholds fell. Witch's covens and occult groups moved out of the area, finding they could no longer function in the territory.

Today, our county is one of the top revenue producers in the State of Florida and one of the fastest growing counties in the United States. Our schools rank second in the state. Our law enforcement is the model agency for the state, as is our business community and Chamber of Commerce.

None of this could have been accomplished without the dedication, cooperation and alignment of our teams and team leaders.

Alignment brings new assignments and the power to accomplish great things for the Kingdom of God. I encourage you to search your heart and ask the Lord to show you any areas that are misaligned and affecting your personal places of growth; also, any areas that need new alignments so you are better equipped to accomplish every new assignment God brings your way.

6

The Church Aligned

MODERN CHRISTIANS TEND TO AVOID ALIGNMENT. This is especially true in the Charismatic and Kingdom churches. With the teaching on individual empowerment through the Holy Spirit, coupled with media-fed frenzies over the moral failures of prominent church leaders, today's Christian treats God like a slot machine: one hand on the Bible, the other on the handle, pulling in faith for the cherries to align and the treasure to spill forth. Would that it was that easy. It's not.

In all fairness to the present generation, many people are under the power of personal prophecy that promotes grandiose visions of spiritual conquest.

"I don't know how I'm seeing this," says the "prophet" to the single mother of six young children. "But God's showing me that you are going to be a missionary to China. And...*what's that, Lord? Oh, OK*.... You are in a golden chariot, and each of your children is in a smaller chariot, and they are being pulled by the leaders of the Chinese government! Glory to God! Sell your house and buy your tickets!"

It doesn't take much to get people confused these days. They tend to build their future hopes on questionable prophetic words given to them by people prophesying what they want to hear. The right word coupled with the wrong interpretation can spell big trouble. Of course, the wrong word coupled with any interpretation (other than: *this is baloney!*) won't be any better.

Timing is everything. Sometimes, people move too quickly on a prophetic word. I still have prophecies that were given to me in 1984 when I was locked in a prayer closet for five months and had three visitations from Jesus. Some things have not come to pass yet. I have a lot to look forward to. (Actually, it was four visitations. The last one was: "Clay, come out of the prayer closet.")

Alignment with authentic leadership in a Spirit-led church body leads to purity of truth. But don't just take my word for it. Here's what Solomon—the smartest person in the world—has to say. (I think he was from Arkansas.)

> *Where there is no guidance the people fall,*
> *But in an abundance of counselors there is victory.*
> Proverbs 11:14
> *Without consultation, plans are frustrated,*
> *But with many counselors they succeed.*
> Provers 15:22
> *For by wise guidance you will wage war,*
> *And in an abundance of counselors there is victory.*
> Proverbs 24:6

In the right environment, people tend to congregate, join together and align. It is the natural state of mankind as created by God. Which begs the question: why even teach on alignment if people are going to do it anyway? Well, the answer is: we don't live in the right environment. We live in a world imbued with sin. As Paul told us in Romans 5:12:

> *Therefore, just as through one man sin entered into the world, and death through sin, and so death spread to all mankind, because all sinned.*

The forces opposed to our alignment are legion. The devil knows that what divides us eventually conquers us. So, he does all in his power to separate us. Jesus observed this when he said:

> *Every kingdom divided against itself is laid waste; and no city or house divided against itself will stand.*
>
> Matthew 12:25

Alignment with authentic leadership in a Spirit-led church body leads to purity of truth.

Alignment is warfare. The time spent together, sharing a drink or building a barn, cooking a meal or hiking on a gorgeous fall afternoon, builds relationship and opposes the schemes of the enemy.

Nothing in God is complicated.

It's our flesh, working through the power of sin, that makes an impossible obstacle from what is natural. When Paul observed that "the wages of sin is death" (Romans 6:23), he was identifying a process by which people die slowly...over time...which is why they don't notice.

We tend to separate from other people at the least provocation. Unfortunately, what feels like liberation on the day we storm off to drive our stake into the beachhead of isolation soon becomes the killing field upon which enemy snipers use us for target practice. Aligned, we stand; isolated, we fall.

Nothing in God is complicated.

People often isolate due to trauma. The loneliest person in the darkest cave yearns for contact, but the scars from previous attempts keep the entrance obscured. Without intentionally focusing on alignment, we tend to splinter, and once splintered, the trauma keeps us apart. I had a friend who used to say: "I've had two marriages in my life. My first...and my last!"

We have to be intentional on addressing the corrosive power of sin. Ignoring it and hoping it will go away is not a strategy; it's a surrender.

Let us remember that on the day of Pentecost, Holy Spirit did not come to separate individuals. Holy Spirit came to a group of believers, 120 of them, who were "all together in one place" (Acts 2:1). They had been praying for many days, seeking one thing: the power that Jesus promised:

You will receive power when the Holy Spirit has come upon you; and you shall be My witnesses both in Jerusalem and in all Judea, and Samaria, and as far as the remotest part of the earth.

Acts 1:8

They were aligned; they were one; and the power to launch the Christian church fell upon them all as foretold by the prophet Joel:

"It will come about after this
That I will pour out My Spirit on all mankind;
And your sons and your daughters will prophesy,
Your old men will have dreams,
Your young men will see visions.

Joel: 2:28

"All mankind…." Aligned, fitly joined together with integrity. Were God to give it in the same measure to isolated individuals, it would destroy them. The power of God flows through alignment, and that is through relationship.

This is not to say that people of God cannot operate alone. Some are called to individual functions, but most are not. We can think of it like Paul's life of celibacy: it's the gift that everyone admires but nobody wants. The fact is, an aligned church operates in greater power, overcomes greater obstacles, endures tougher times together, celebrates good times with gusto, and generally does life in the true sense of community.

The Church Aligned

An unaligned church still operates with power, but much of it is personally directed energy, and that is used in forcing agreement and fending off discord. An unaligned church considers it a triumph when everyone sings from the same page of the hymnal. They still pray, but the prayers are for establishing the fellowship, not conquering a sin-ravaged world. Their focus is internal. They are that broken body in the hospital bed, arms and legs in traction, fighting for healing. This is not a body from which you expect anything requiring real effort. They revel in the psalm: "Behold, how good and how pleasant it is for brothers to live together in unity!" (Psalm 133:1). But they compromise to the lowest common denominator to achieve that unity.

This is why Hebrews implores us:

Let's consider how to encourage one another in love and good deeds, not abandoning our own meeting together, as is the habit of some people, but encouraging one another; and all the more as you see the day drawing near.

Hebrews 10:24-25

No, this is not to get people into the church so the offerings are good. It's to get people into the power of agreement so their lives are victorious.

When Ezekial stood over a valley of dry bones, scattered about the desert, bleached white from the sun, all flesh picked clean by the bugs and birds that cleanse the rot from the earth, he prophesied and the bones responded:

So I prophesied as I was commanded; and as I prophesied, there was a loud noise, and behold, a rattling; and the bones came together, bone to its bone. And I looked, and behold, tendons were on them, and flesh grew and skin covered them; but there was no breath in them. Then He said to me, "Prophesy to the breath, prophesy, son of man, and say to the breath, 'The Lord God says this: "Come from the four winds, breath, and breathe on these slain, so that they come to life." So I prophesied as He commanded me, and the breath entered them, and they came to life and stood on their feet, an exceedingly great army.

Ezekiel 37:7-10

Notice the progression here: the bones were in pieces, then they came together; tendons and flesh joined them; and when they aligned, the breath of life came into them. They stood and became an "exceedingly great army." An aligned church is an exceedingly great army.

The bones were not empowered; only the alignment of the bones was empowered. Such is the church today: some bones, some sinews, and some aligned. And if that gives you cause for reflection, consider one more observation: How did the bones end up in the valley in the first place? They were alive at one point. What happened to them?

The wages of our isolation are …?

Unhealthy Progression

If a person abruptly leaves a church position because they have an invitation to be on the leadership team of another church, chances are, it's not God. That's not how God works. If another leader starts luring people out of churches to build theirs, they are operating like the thief spoken of in John:

Truly, truly I say to you, the one who does not enter by the door into the fold of the sheep, but climbs up some other way, he is a thief and a robber.

John 10:1

Certainly, people change churches for a variety of reasons; some noble, some not so noble. The key is communication between both leaders and the person in question. Alignment must be respected. The condition in which a person leaves a church determines the condition in which they will enter their next church.

Never forfeit a divinely aligned relationship for a quick promotion. People may think they are going on to bigger and better things, but unless they leave properly, they are merely perpetuating their personal dysfunction. Likewise, the way a leader builds a church determines the outcome. Violating God's alignment will poison any future relationships and doom the new leader's prospects of building a sustainable body of believers. It all starts with alignment.

Honoring Alignment

When my daughters were first married, they needed help financially. Naturally, they called Susan, and she relayed the message to me. Now, in those days, I was pretty tough-minded. Nobody got the best of Clay Nash. Nosiree! You wanted something; you earned it.

So, when Susan told me of their struggles, I had a terse answer:

"Will a check do?"

Yeah, well…they're my daughters. *Know what I mean?* When they didn't think I was listening, they called me Daddy Deep Pockets.

Anyway, one day, Susan called me and said,

"One of your daughters needs three hundred dollars. Their car broke down and they need to get it fixed."

"Give her the money," I said.

A little while later, the Lord said to me, "You're a thief and robber."

"Lord, I ain't stole nothing," I pleaded.

"Giving her that money…you're a thief and a robber."

"How's that, Sir?"

"You're not going through her husband, who is the gate into that sheepfold. You need to know they are no longer your daughters. They are those men's wives. And the covenant between a husband and wife is far greater than a father and a daughter."

> *Alignment. Respect it, and there is prosperity. Violate it, and there is poverty.*

Well, he took me to the woodshed. I asked Susan, "Whichever one it was, have her husband call me."

And so, we started going through the husband. You know what? Very quickly they didn't need our help. They started prospering. The Lord showed me: "Every time you didn't go through the gate, giving them money was like putting it in a sack that had a hole in the corner. You are giving the cankerworm entitlement to eat of that which you were blessing with. You were enabling the enemy to continue to cycle in their life."

Alignment. Respect it, and there is prosperity. Violate it, and there is poverty.

Principles of Alignment

Here are three principles of alignment that have stood the test of time.

1. <u>Anyone who is unwilling to submit to authority is not worthy to be followed because they're not properly aligned.</u>

The authority of alignment in our lives brings great safety. It has saved my ministry when we were attacked with false accusations. My apostolic alignment group met with me—those leaders with whom I am aligned—and I was completely exonerated.

Alignment means we are already established in relationships that uphold us, challenge us, investigate us and if necessary, correct us. That way, when trouble comes—notice: I did not say *if* trouble comes—our network is already up and running. It's like the guy whose house was invaded by robbers, and he ran to the garage and began lifting weights.

Too late, buddy. The time to build your relational alignments is before the challenges, the obstacles, the perplexing conundrums that afflict us all. Certainly, our relationships deepen through tough times, but having them established early is vital. It's too late to think about building a boat as you cascade over Niagara Falls. (Hopefully, you left the keys in the truck.)

Comfort can be deceiving; nothing lulls us into false security like success. I recently asked someone, "Who are you accountable to? Who are you aligned with?"

"Well," they said. "I've kind of reached a place where I don't need accountability. I'm doing just fine on my own."

"Then, I don't think you and I are going to walk very far together," I replied. "I'll be your friend, but I can't build with you. Because if we get into a disagreement, I've got no one to go to."

As the Apostle in our church, I am still accountable to our elders. My elders know they can come and talk to me at the foot of the cross; that is ground level. But if I don't agree with them, they know they have the right to contact those above me to whom I am accountable.

It's a matter of degrees of correction. A church body thrives in alignment. Power, authority and accountability flow from this relationship. However, when difficulties arise that are beyond the ability of the local body to overcome, that's when the alignment of leaders is brought to bear. I'm already aligned with those leaders; they know me and trust me, as do I them, so correction or validation flows much easier.

2. <u>When authentic alignment is in place, responsibility will be motivated by love.</u>

I love being in alignment with the leadership of NEI. I love walking with my fellow leaders. I submit to alignment out of love; that is my motivation. Authentic alignment cannot be motivated by insecurity, greed or self-aggrandizing. If you are in alignment with leadership, you can only have one motivation: respect through love. All others must be dealt with as they come up. No one is perfect; people may have many things in their hearts when they seek alignment, but the end goal is to serve one another in love.

Years ago, I built a great eldership in a church in Dyersburg; we had five elders. For whatever reason, there was a lot of lawlessness in the church. It seemed like every elder's meeting dealt with a sin problem. We grew into disliking each other. I didn't want to be in the room with them. It felt like I was always dealing with their problems. One of my elders felt it too.

"Look, something's wrong," he said. "I'm getting to where I don't even like you guys."

We stopped and reassessed. We realized we were only coming together to deal with problems. We decided to change course, to find a new motive for gathering. So, once a month we got together and played volleyball, had a barbecue, and hung out with each other. Gradually, we rebuilt the positive dynamics that drew us together in the first place. In a sense, we cleaved unto each other. In time, the issues we had to deal with didn't seem nearly as draining. Anybody can pay the bills where there is money in the bank. Once we began investing in our relationships, the challenges were easy.

3. <u>Authentic alignment is established through obedience but it's validated through the choice to trust.</u>

Notice my words here: *choice* of trust. Most people have been taught that trust is earned. Well, trust is not earned; it's a choice. It starts small; nobody trusts completely right away. But there has to be a start, and that is a decision point. You are either going to extend trust or you're not. If you do, and that trust is validated, respect will be established, leading to greater trust. "The journey of a thousand miles begins…with trust."

People who experience a bad relationship early in life have a difficult time choosing to trust their present spouse. In counseling, I try to get to the heart of the distrust; it has little to do with the current spouse. Here is a typical exchange:

"Has he ever done anything to make you distrust him? Has he ever come home late? Have you ever seen anything suspicious?"

"I know he's been unfaithful," replies the wife.

Her husband is in the room with us. I ask him to hand me his phone. No problem; he hands it over. Nothing unusual on the phone. No salacious texts, no porn, no questionable web addresses. There isn't even a password on the phone. I show all this to the wife.

"Look here. That's a good sign right there," I said. "No password."

Faced with evidence that runs counter to her dark feelings, she faces a decision: trust and continue in the marriage, or ignore facts and leave him. If she trusts, she will give the husband the chance to prove that her concerns are unfounded.

Trust is tricky with damaged people. Trying to earn it with someone predisposed to not trust is impossible. It really comes down to choice. Trust engenders trust, and trust validated becomes respect, leading to greater trust.

Susan and I have worked hard to trust and establish respect. Personally, I don't have a password on my phone. Susan can pick it up anytime and examine it, but she doesn't. Still, I desire to avoid everything that even looks like evil (ref. 1 Thessalonians 5:22)

I wear a wedding ring, but sometimes my skin gets a rash and I have to stop wearing it for a while. I've had somebody say, "You having problems in your marriage?"

"No, why would you say that?"

"Well, I notice you haven't had a ring on the last two times I've seen you."

"Well, let me tell you: if you can't tell I'm married by now, you don't know me at all. I'm married forever…for two reasons. First, I love her. Second, she's an expert shot with a revolver."

Cathy Lechner, a prophet out of Florida, wrote the book: *Couldn't We Just Kill Em And Tell God They Died?* That's Susan's attitude. I don't mess with her.

> *Trust, respect, and a loaded revolver. Now that's a happy marriage.*

Trust, respect, and a loaded revolver. Now that's a happy marriage.

Alignment and Authority

Alignment is about being recognized, included and respected so we can be empowered. Most people want to be empowered to do what God has put in their hearts. This is not just in ministry, but in all walks of life. If you're in business, get in alignment with the apostolic. It will empower you. We commissioned a businessman at one of the NEI meetings to have his own business. Months later, he told me, "I remember when you decreed over us. I remember what it did. I went to bed that night a midget and woke up the next morning a giant."

Here's how it works:

- When we align with *those leading us*, we are recognized.
- When we align with *those equal to us*, we are included.
- When we align with *those following us*, we are respected.

Each level bestows authority through relationship. Through alignment, our authority is recognized, included, and respected, and we become empowered by God.

7

The Power of Agreement

Again I say to you, that if two of you agree on earth about anything that they may ask, it shall be done for them by My Father who is in heaven. For where two or three have gathered together in My name, I am there in their midst.

Matthew 18:19-20

PEOPLE GET MARRIED FOR MANY REASONS. They're in love. They're lonely. Their biological clock is ticking. All these are good reasons, but none are *the sole* reason for marriage.

Marriage is for alignment. It's an agreement formalizing an inner vow to join your life to another. Like all things in alignment, it is essentially relational, although at first, it can seem like many things. In the beginning, a couple may fight; they may compete; they may seclude themselves for a week in the honeymoon suite of the Waldorf Astoria and live on cold pizza.

Not everything in life is a choice. Eventually, challenges will come that the couple did not foresee. The pleasure will evaporate. The giant will appear. Trust will be broken. Harmony will devolve. The wolf will be at the door. Welcome to the human race; we are all works in progress under our heavenly Father. If we are unprepared, we will think love is gone and life is ruined, but that's not true. Life is merely obscured by the shadow of the evil towering over us. Slay it, and the view will improve considerably. Run, however, and we will find ourselves in greater darkness, up against bigger giants.

In truth, our greatest nemesis is ourselves, that is, our flesh—that part of us still corrupted by sin. How we can run from ourselves? The greatest battle is within; it follows us everywhere and gets stronger through our neglect.

Eventually, every successful couple learns that to survive, they must get down to the business of doing life together, of discovering who they are as individuals and as a couple. Whether they name it as such, they embark on the task of alignment. As they go, they learn what makes them stronger and what makes them weaker. They learn the power of agreement. They will learn how to bring out the best in themselves. They learn that marriage is not just for comfort or fun or raising children or amassing a staggering 401K. Marriage is for conquest through the power of agreement.

> *Two are better than one,*
> *Because they have a good reward for their labor.*
> *For if they fall, one will lift up his companion.*
> *But woe to him who is alone when he falls,*
> *For he has no one to help him up.*
> *Again, if two lie down together, they will keep warm;*
> *But how can one be warm alone?*
> *Though one may be overpowered by another, two can withstand him.*
> *And a threefold cord is not quickly broken.*
> Ecclesiastes 4:9-12

The power of agreement releases things in the spiritual realm. This is why doublemindedness is so destructive; it is the antithesis of the power of agreement. Not only does it fail to receive the power of God, it also opposes the power of God. Agreement causes resources to flow into our lives; doublemindedness causes us to squander the resources we have.

To Conquer Together

When I do a wedding, I am aware that not everyone thinks as I do. Saying "marriage is for conquest" conjures up a host of images; most of them unpleasant. In anticipation of this reaction, I explain that the conquest I speak of is not that of each other; rather, it is:

- to conquer our individual flesh
- to conquer whatever comes against us
- to conquer whatever opposes the work of God

This is why, before I agree to do a wedding, I insist on:

- pre-marital counseling
- using the vows (based on Kenneth Copeland's vows)
- a prophetic presbytery
- a place in the ceremony to speak on the power of agreement.

My aim is not just to teach the couple; if they've had my counseling, they should know these principles before the wedding day. My teaching is for the congregation in attendance. They are the witnesses for eternity.

When time permits, I also take both sets of in-laws through pre-marriage counseling. I remind them that Adam and Eve were instructed to let a man leave and cleave. Adam's father was Father God, and God was establishing precedence to honor the alignment between a husband and wife.

> *Therefore shall a man leave his father and his mother, and shall cleave unto his wife: and they shall be one flesh.*
>
> Genesis 2:24

"Cleave unto his wife." The word *cleave* has a dual meaning. A butcher's cleaver divides, but to cleave also means "to cling, to adhere, to abide fast together, to follow." When the alignment of marriage is respected, the couple grows together. Yet when it's mishandled, you're dead meat.

God brings people into alignment because, through the power of agreement, they are stronger than individuals working separately. Alignment is the overarching relationship leading to being fitly joined together, each joint supplying what is needed. Agreement is the power found within alignment. This is what Amos meant when he asked: "Can two walk together, unless they are agreed?" (Amos 3:3).

Alignment is the power to conquer, as Paul tells us in Romans chapter 8:37-39

> *But in all these things we overwhelmingly conquer through Him who loved us. For I am convinced that neither death, nor life, nor angels, nor principalities, nor things present, nor things to come, nor powers, nor height, nor depth, nor any other created thing will be able to separate us from the love of God that is in Christ Jesus our Lord.*

Many good people are busily engaged, trying to accomplish the assignments God has called them to, but they're not able to complete them because they lack alignment with other people and organizations that God uses to empower ministries. The fact is, most assignments are not for individuals alone but require the synergy that comes through alignment with others.

When we read the Bible through an American worldview, it seems full of rugged individuals performing godly heroics. Yet through a Hebraic perspective, we gain a different perspective.

- Noah did not build the ark alone. *His family worked with him.*
- Moses did not stand before Pharoah alone. *Aaron stood with him.*
- David led an army of misfits to reclaim the throne. *Too many giants for one sling.*
- Nehimiah organized labor to rebuild the wall of Jerusalem. *I think it was the Teamsters.*

Yes, God has his pioneers, but these are often trained by organizations, supplied and sent out by organizations, and later supported by organization. Interestingly, the first thing that happens, after a pioneer breaks through opposition and establishes a toehold in a new land, is they attract a following.

If mankind was designed to function alone, there would not have been an Adam and Eve. It would have just been Adam, alone in the garden, wondering why the animals got to have all the fun on Saturday night.

Called and Chosen

Christians are taught: "With the calling comes the equipping." Another way to say it is: "Whom God calls, he equips." Yes, these are true, but like all sayings, they gloss over some important details. There is a process involved; the calling is only the first step.

The Lord's grace for an assignment flows through alignment. This is vital. Without alignment—and the maturation that occurs—the assignment could destroy us. Until we are fully equipped for the task ahead, attempting it alone is foolish at best, fatal at worst. Alignment with others is a crucial part of being equipped. Sure, it might not seem that way when we first start out. We are brimming with promise, eager to try our wings. *As optimistic as a newly minted pastor*. It's when things go wrong that we realize our need for alignment, and not just any alignment, but the alignment for the present hour.

Godly alignment brings us together with people who have what we need; people with authority, a righteous history, a proven record. These are people who are trustworthy, honorable and operate with integrity. Alignment with others proves us, tests us and prepares us for success. God is not in the business of failure. He is not out to expose our sins to make us grovel about, bemoaning our lot and professing our utter dependency on him. As righteous as this may sound to those of a religious mindset, God wants to bring us to where we can perform at the level he expects.

> *The Lord's grace for an assignment flows through alignment. This is vital.*

God is in the business of success, and everything he requires is focused on that success. Alignment equips us for success.

When you align with an apostolic ministry, you are positioned according to your calling. The apostolic anointing is about positioning people, but it's also about equipping people in that position. One of the greatest things a minister can do is to help you become who you are. God's grace empowers us; that is widely understood. What is less understood is that it empowers us to be *who we really are*.

I was amazed when our first child, Dawn, would cry. Susan would say, "She's hungry," and she would feed her. Then two hours later, she'd cry again and Susan would say, "She needs to be changed," and she would change her. Then two hours after that, she'd cry and Susan would say, "She wants to be held," and she would hold her.

It sounded like the same crying to me. Why was that? It's because God graces a mother with intuition and insight that the dad rarely has. Susan's position was mother; her equipping was knowing her baby's needs. She was good at it, thank God!

When you align with an apostolic ministry, it positions you for ministry, then helps you discover the grace God has given you—the power of God that flows with your God-given nature.

Jesus said, "Many are called but few are chosen" (Matthew 22:14). He was describing a selection process, and it serves as a reality check. Yes, aligning with an apostolic ministry is vital to fulfilling a calling, but it is not a guarantee that we will be chosen. Here are the facts: not everyone makes it in everything. If you are not chosen, do not expect God's empowerment, and do not launch yourself without it.

Many things can be done through youthful exuberance; endurance is not one of them.

Alignment Is Relational

The things that bring you the most joy in relational alignment are indications of your God-given purpose to fulfill your destiny.

We enjoy the things we are passionate about. It's never taxing. The writer of Hebrews said, "Let us labor therefore to enter into that rest" (Hebrews 4:11 KJV). He was speaking about finding that thing that God created you for—your original intent. Successful people find their passion and pursue it. The worst place in life is to be doing something merely because you have to do it. In the movie, *The Rookie,* Dennis Quaid made a great statement. "Your grandfather once told me it was ok to think about what you want to do until it was time to start doing what you were meant to do."

When God tests you to see if you will do something, it's not about getting that thing done; it's about showing you what you were really meant to do.

When I began to work under Don Stewart, he had bought an old cargo van. We took bus seats from a junk bus and bolted them onto the floor and used it to carry a wild bunch of cursing teenagers to church. Now, I've been pretty heathen in my B.C. days (Before Christ), but I heard language in that van that made the paint blister. Every week, they would tear the seats out of the van, and I'd have to bolt them back in. Looking back on it, God was testing me. In so doing, he was bringing me to that place of discovering what I was passionate about.

When I moved to Southaven, Mississippi, based on a word from John Paul Jackson, I asked the Lord a question. "Lord, why another church?"

"Because I don't want you to teach people how to be committed to me," he said. "I want you to teach people how to enjoy me."

That's all he said; he didn't give me any more, which is probably a good thing, because I didn't really understand what he was saying anyway. But a few months after that, we got a major snow for that area—eight inches worth! Our house had a steep driveway, so like every good Southerner, I headed to Walmart for a snow shovel and salt so I could get up the driveway. On the way, I saw four men on a golf course. They were playing golf in the snow. *Those idiots!*

Now, if you're a golfer, forgive me, but you probably understand those men. I don't know much about golf. I play with my grandkids at putt-putt golf, but that's about it. I discovered that guys who play in the snow don't play with a white ball. Good thing. They play with a fluorescent ball. That made sense. What made even more sense was when the Lord showed me that what you enjoy, you're committed to.

Even though I couldn't understand golfing in eight inches of snow, I guided duck hunting for eleven years and never missed a morning. I got up hours before sunrise, gulped down a large coffee, and found my way with blurry eyes to the duck blind where I'd hunker down in the cold, hoping for a flock of ducks to appear above me. I enjoyed that. At least I didn't have to swing at a little glowing ball.

God's point was simple: find those things that stir passion in you, then seek alignment with those who appreciate that passion, and allow them to develop your skills. In the process of finding what you enjoy, you'll find the commitment to do it.

Alignment is Neutral

Scripture tells us:

> *My people are destroyed for lack of knowledge.*
> *Since you have rejected knowledge,*
> *I also will reject you from being My priest.*
> *Since you have forgotten the Law of your God,*
> *I also will forget your children.*
>
> Hosea 4:6

The Power of Agreement

Ignorance of how alignment works will destroy alignment. It's not what you might think.

****

Years ago, Hurricane Katrina hit New Orleans and destroyed the levee system that was designed to keep millions of gallons of seawater at bay. The result was the flooding of hundreds of miles of Louisiana real estate and the loss of thousands of homes. It took years to redesign and restore the levees.

The land along the Mississippi River is some of the most fertile soil in the nation. It got that way from the flooding that occurred each year when the river would overcome the banks and flood the surrounding fields and forest.

When we align with someone, our strengths flow together. Where they have strength, we have needs, just as our strengths supply their needs. That much is good. But that's not the entire process.

Our weaknesses also have access to one another. Alignment brings two or more people together, period. Hopefully, they both do so with the goal of synergy: making the two greater than one-plus-one. If they are not vigilant, however, they may acquire traits that are not beneficial, especially if they admire the person with whom they are aligning.

Leaders are not perfect; they are appointed. Most leaders I know are powerful in their positions, but vastly ill-suited for other positions. We are fit for purpose; we operate well where we belong. We don't operate well where we don't belong.

Alignment is neutral. It doesn't care what passes between two or more people. It is like the internet; it merely brokers the exchange.

When two people marry, it isn't long before they take stock of one another—an honest appraisal of the person they gave their lives to. Sometimes, that examination brings a shock. Realizing that they are aligned with weaknesses in certain areas can be troubling. If they are joined in the bond of love, however, they will be motivated to help each other. One supplies...the other needs. Essentially, they develop strength in the areas where the other one struggles, and that becomes the needed supply.

A woman may not be the greatest with budgeting, but if she realizes that her husband cannot even do simple math, she might read a book on organizing family finances and take over the checkbook.

A man could have no experience in cooking, but if his wife constantly burns water, he might enroll in a James Beard cooking class to keep the family from starving. Who knows? He just might find that he likes pulling a perfect spinach quiche from the oven and serving it with fresh baked sourdough bread.

We develop strengths where the other is weak. This is how synergy is made.

In contrast, if we are not joined in love, we might come to resent the weakness in the other. Rather than offer our supply—what we have or what we can develop—we sulk and fume and withhold more of ourselves, seeking to punish the other person for their lack. *That's a recipe for success, now isn't it?* Gradually, the relationship devolves until both people are weaker than they were alone. This is the opposite of synergy; it is a contagion, and it slowly kills a relationship.

Paul understood the dynamics of alignment when he wrote to the Corinthians:

> *Do not be mismatched with unbelievers; for what do righteousness and lawlessness share together, or what does light have in common with darkness? Or what harmony does Christ have with Belial, or what does a believer share with an unbeliever? Or what agreement does the temple of God have with idols?*
>
> 2 Corinthians 6:14-16

Now, I realize this is a bit harsh. Hopefully, the one we align with is not a devil worshiper. But the principle is the same. Being yoked together is a form of alignment; it's when two people come together for a common purpose. We find it everywhere: in marriage, in occupations, in ministry; anywhere two or more people put their hands to the proverbial plow, there is alignment. The transaction that results affects both people. The other person may not be evil; most likely they are not evil. They may simply not be the right fit for you.

Work around a group of negative people long enough and you will start to feel as they do. Minister with people of a certain mindset regarding Holy Spirit, the Kingdom of God, prayer, fasting, and your thinking will shift. Marry 700 wives whose gods are not the Lord, and….well, ask Solomon.

> Now *King Solomon loved many foreign women* along with the daughter of Pharaoh: Moabite, Ammonite, Edomite, Sidonian, and Hittite women, from the nations of which the Lord had said to the sons of Israel, "*You shall not associate with them, nor shall they associate with you; they will certainly turn your heart away to follow their gods.*"
>
> Solomon clung to these in love.
>
> For when Solomon was old, *his wives turned his heart away to follow other gods*; and his heart was not wholly devoted to the Lord his God, as the heart of his father David had been. For Solomon became a follower of Ashtoreth the goddess of the Sidonians, and of Milcom the abhorrent idol of the Ammonites.
>
> So *Solomon did what was evil in the sight of the Lord,* and did not follow the Lord fully, as his father David had done.
>
> 1 Kings 11:1-2, 4-6

Who we associate with influences us. Alignment is at the heart of that influence. Solomon loved his wives, and they turned his heart.

Love removes barriers. Love lowers our guard. Love takes down our levees, and the sea water rushes into our fresh water reservoir. See?

Solomon would have done well to heed the words of Proverbs:

> *Watch over your heart with all diligence,*
> *For from it flow the springs of life.*
>
> Proverbs 4:23

Come to think of it, he wrote these words. Perhaps he should have read Paul's advice to his spiritual son Timothy:

> *Holding to a form of godliness although they have denied its power; <u>avoid such people</u> as these.*
>
> 2 Timothy 3:5

8

Unity and Oneness

ONE OF JESUS' FINAL PRAYERS on earth was recorded by John. His prayer came down to a profound utterance, pleading for those he was leaving behind.

> *I do not pray for these alone, but also for those who will believe in Me through their word; that they all may <u>be one</u>, as You, Father, are in Me, and I in You; that they also may <u>be one</u> in Us, that the world may believe that You sent Me. And the glory which You gave Me I have given them, that they may <u>be one</u> just as We <u>are one</u>: I in them, and You in Me; that they may be made perfect <u>in one</u>, and that the world may know that You have sent Me, and have loved them as You have loved Me.*
>
> John 17:20-23

Jesus prayed for his believers to be one—one with the Father, one with himself, and one among themselves. From this alignment, they would know the love of the Father, and the world would know that Jesus was sent by the Father. Thus, the same love that Jesus enjoyed would be shared by all who believed in him.

This was a powerful moment; his passion for mankind was the source of his enduring joy, the same that carried him through all he would suffer for the next several hours.

> *Looking only at Jesus, the originator and perfecter of the faith, <u>who for the joy set before Him endured the cross</u>, despising the shame, and has sat down at the right hand of the throne of God.*
>
> Hebrews 12:2

Jesus endured the cross in the hope of believers sharing the love of the Father.

It is important to understand oneness. Unity and oneness are not synonymous. Unity is a process that leads to becoming one. Unity builds upon an event. Oneness transcends the event to establish relational spiritual alignment.

Unity happens on many levels. People in church buildings are unified in that they are in the same location, in the same seats, watching the same clock, wondering if the same speaker is going to give the same longwinded sermon as every other Sunday. That's unity; it's not oneness.

When Ezekiel saw the valley of bones, they were unified. The bones were in the same place, in the same condition: unaligned and unproductive. They were unified but they weren't fit for purpose until they came together, bone to bone, and the Spirit of God breathed on them. That's when they achieved oneness; that's when they became aligned.

Aligned with Values

Alignment for conquest is far greater than being part of an organization. It's being joined together with other people at a heart level. You learn to share their values and perspectives.

Unity and Oneness

When we came to CityGate church in Southaven, MS, there were two couples in the church who were friends of ours. They both told me, "We don't want to hurt your feelings, Clay, but we're not coming. We're out with church. We just don't do church anymore."

Well, twenty years later, they're leaders in CityGate, and they are thriving. Here's how that happened.

The husband came and sat with me. He's a New York Italian. He and his wife were both raised on Long Island. He wanted to feel me out a bit on certain things near and dear to the heart of an Italian.

"How do you feel about drinking wine?" he asked.

"That depends. I need to understand the purpose of your question," I answered.

"Well, I want to know what your values are about. Do you believe that, as a minister, you can't drink wine? What do you believe?"

"I believe that you can…in moderation."

"Okay," he said. "The last pastor we sat under was a teetotaler. He didn't believe in any form of consumption, and we quit drinking wine…not because the pastor asked us to, but because we valued the pastor's values."

"Well, I like a good steak and a nice glass of wine once in a while."

"That's good. So we can have some good wine with our manicotti!"

"Wait a minute! Only if you bring me some manicotti, all right?"

They made the best manicotti I've ever had.

The true test of whether you're in alignment with someone is whether or not you can value their values.

I traveled all over Europe with one of my spiritual fathers, Warwick Shenton, who is now with the Lord. Warwick was a teetotaler. Now, in Europe, they're going to serve you wine. I'm telling you: it's going to happen. However, I would never consume any because of his values, and that was my choosing. I discovered that valuing the same things is very important to alignment.

God is looking to bring us into alignment to where we begin to function as one.

We can't be in relational covenant with people who don't share our values. As one who works with the tithes and offerings that God's people bring to the church, I value their giving as much as the devil fears it. As a minister who looks after the flock, I have seen the positive results of giving just as I have seen the destructive results of not giving. This is not a get-rich scheme, not for the givers or the leadership. Rather, it is the fulfillment of scripture that tells us to bring the tithe to the storehouse to rebuke the devourer. It's for the protection of God's people as much as it is for the furtherance of the Kingdom of God. Therefore, I teach on the importance of first fruits giving and tithing to cause the body to function fitly joined together as His church.

We can't be in relational covenant with people who don't share our values.

If a leader who did not share our values on giving came to our gathering, I could not align with that person. We could remain friends, but alignment would be impossible.

Values in Marriage

I married Susan because I loved her. But I also married her because my mother and dad divorced when I was twelve and I was tired of eating El Patio frozen TV dinners. Over the years, we've discovered many more dynamics of why God brought us together. She's my bedrock. She's the strength I need. I could not function without her.

Today, I value her values. It wasn't always like that. Years ago, God told me:

"I want you to start valuing the things that Susan values."

"Lord, like what?"

"She likes to shop. I want you to go shopping with her."

"Lord, is this purgatory?"

Well, I started going to the supermarket with her. I pushed the grocery cart and she perused the shelves. In time, I understood why Susan liked to shop. It was her way of providing for her family. She looked for the best quality, the best deals, to share with me and the children. Shopping was an extension of her loving heart. How could I not value that? It was a beautiful thing to behold, and it brought us closer.

Oneness

One of the closest people to me was my father, Bob Nash. We had a oneness that has never been rivaled by any other man. I've had people tell me my relationship with him actually intimidated them. They didn't understand it. I didn't care. I learned a lot about life from him. That can never be replaced.

At one time, my father and I owned several corporations, and a lot of it was based on large farm equipment. We're a very mechanically inclined family. My grandson, Logan, at 13, could repair a four-wheeler, lay it out like it'll never run again, and put it back together better than new. His dad didn't teach him that. I didn't teach him that. It was imparted to him; it's in his DNA. (He's also a bit onery at times; I'm sure he got that from Susan.)

Impartation only comes through alignment. My dad never sat me down and said, "Boy, I'm going to teach you how to overhaul an engine." Instead, I watched my dad; I worked with my dad. He made me pay attention. I couldn't be wandering off on my own, gazing at barn owls, wondering how they built those nests in the rafters. I had to focus. After being around him a little bit, he would say, "Clay, hand me a three-quarter-inch wrench."

At first, I had questions. *Where are the wrenches? What's three-quarter-inch mean?* In time, I got very good at it. The moment I heard "Hand me...," I'd place it in his palm—the right wrench, at the right time, in the right direction. By focusing on him, we became one, and I learned almost everything he knew.

When Susan and I were first married, Dad would come over to our house early in the morning and have coffee with us. While Susan listened in amazement, the conversation would go something like this:

"Hey Clay, you know, the Smith's cow—"

"—got hit last night by a pickup. Yeah, Dad."

"I wish I'd have been there, but—"

"—Smith's too cheap to—"

"—give away any meat anyhow."

Susan and I laugh because now we do that. As a married couple, we have become one, finishing each other's sentences.

Join the Team

Alignment is not a religious term. Too many people think they are building alignment but all they're really doing is recruiting people under a common banner: *If you're not aligned with us, you're really not aligned.* At best, they are building unity. At worst, they are creating a religious organization with themselves at the top.

Each individual must discover their God-given purpose, then find alignment that fits and honors that alignment. The alignment that one person has with a leader or organization might not be the alignment for you. Search it out. Seek God's leading. Remember: your God-given grace will flow with your personality; it's vital that you learn who you are.

One of the greatest times of any church is when they go into a building program because they move from being unified to being one.

We're building a new building! We're adding on to the building. We remodeling! Everybody dig in! Grab a shovel and get to work!

Unlike many of the more ethereal aims of ministry, a building project is a tangible goal, a reality that everyone can see and (hopefully) agree upon. Often, lack of oneness in a church or organization is not because people don't believe; it's because they don't share a common vision. "Without a vision, the people perish" (Proverbs 29:18 KJV).

When we started CityGate in Southaven, MS, we struggled to achieve any spiritual breakthrough. Then we decided to remodel the sanctuary. I got people together and we painted together, changed out all the lights from fluorescent to canned lights so that we could dim them. We worked hard. People showed up after work and stayed until 11 pm. Men and women pitched in equally. People brought food. One lady rewired all the lights on a 30-foot scissor lift. Her father was an electrician; she did him proud.

In the process, we moved from being unified as a church to achieving oneness. God wants us to become one.

Aligned With God

When Susan and I first heard leaders like Brother Hagen or Oral Roberts teach on the power of agreement, we didn't understand it. I thought being in agreement meant Susan doing what I said. (So much for that plan.) We slipped off a few roads and got stuck in some ditches a few times. We spent some nights talking to each other in passionate tones until the wee hours of the morning. Well, I hope it was passion; it certainly was LOUD passion (and I spent the night on the couch). But we never let the sun go down on our anger. In the process, we discovered that if Susan aligned with what God said, and if I aligned with what God said, it put us in alignment with each other. When she and I became one with what God said, we became one with each other.

When I do marriage counseling today, I have the couple imagine they are in opposite corners of the room and Jesus is standing in the middle. My instructions are simple:

"We're not trying to reconcile you to each other. We're not trying to get you connected. We're trying to get each of you connected to Jesus. Husband in this corner; wife in that corner. Now start moving toward Jesus. The closer you get to Jesus, the closer you get to each other. See? It's a natural process. Align with Jesus and you will align with each other."

It worked. A lot of counseling just deals with symptoms; it is designed to get a couple back together under the same roof. But that only reties the same two cats by the same two tails. It doesn't resolve anything. Focusing on Jesus builds the triangle with Jesus at the top and the two married people on either side of the base.

<u>Unity is built upon an event, but becoming one transcends the event and knits people together under God.</u>

As the Body of Christ, we are to be knitted together with our focus on Jesus. In the past, we have tried to find unity in events. The March for Jesus days; the Promise Keepers gatherings; things like this brought unity but not oneness. When you move into oneness, it brings an entirely different dynamic.

Ever seen a quarterback who didn't have the rest of the team behind him? Ever seen a three-point shooter in basketball try to carry the rest of team? One person can do good things, but it takes a team to do great things.

God is moving us out of a *dunamis* ("dynamite") mindset. An exploding stick of dynamite is an event. Once it goes off, it's a constant production of power. But *dunamis* also means "dynamo" as in "engine." Machines turn on a series of contained reactions. Diesel engines explode many times a minute, but the force of those reactions is controlled and directed to useful work. Likewise, God is shifting the church from an event mindset—the next prophet, the next prayer line, the next church with the flashy exterior—to a sustained body. We are moving into that place where we value alignment as God has given it to us. Alignment is about finding the place where you can be fitly joined together and then working there.

People are integrated through alignment for a kingdom purpose.

<u>In unity, people assemble for common interest, but in oneness, people are fitly joined together for kingdom purpose.</u>

A building requires integrity to stand; the trusses fit together; the walls support the trusses; the foundation supports the walls. Anything built without integrity will not stand for long.

> *Everyone who hears these words of Mine, and acts on them, will be like a wise man who built his house on the rock. And the rain fell and the floods came, and the winds blew and slammed against that house; and yet it did not fall, for it had been founded on the rock. And everyone who hears these words of Mine, and does not act on them, will be like a foolish man who built his house on the sand. And the rain fell and the floods came, and the winds blew and slammed against that house; and it fell—and its collapse was great.*
>
> Matthew 7:24-27

I know of a great revival that lasted for 16 months. People got saved. The lame walked. The dumb spoke. And in the end, the revival's leader abandoned his marriage and ran off with another man's wife. How can a person lead a true revival and commit a sin like that at the end? Simple, really. It was built on sand. Anything you build will look good for a while. The faster it is built, the flashier it looks. Until the rains start. Until reality sets in. Until we leave the artificial dichotomy of spirit and the natural and realize that our actions in either realm are reflected in both realms.

Think your ministry is great? *How's your marriage?*

Think you are carrying God's mantle to the darkest corners of the earth? *How well do you know your neighbor?*

Think you are praying down the power of heaven? *When's the last time you talked to your kids?*

The revivals I've been a part of have changed me for the good. I once preached continually for 143 nights. Never missed a night.

It was a small church in the middle of a beanfield in Arkansas. On the first night, a little girl who had been born deaf, was snuck in by her aunt and uncle because her parents, who were Church of Christ, did not want her to come. In the middle of my preaching, her ears opened and she began speaking clearly. She didn't just get a healing; she got a creative miracle of being able to speak. I'm telling you, that little church went from 0 to 60 in 1.4 seconds. The next night, we had so many people in that tiny building that we put 40 people in the choir loft built for 20 people. It was incredible! We went 143 nights with services. But it didn't just change the people; it changed me.

God changes everything he's a part of. As the land in our nation gets healed, we are going to see great things. Years ago, we were told we were close to using up all the oil and gas reserves. Now I read that we have more natural gas in this nation than in any place in the world. Was it always there? Possibly. But it's also possible that as we're healing the land, it's doing what it's supposed to do and producing more.

There is nothing wrong with unifying around an event. If that's all we do, however, we will say goodbye when the event is over and go our separate ways. When people go on a mission trip with strangers, they bond with each other. They learn how to work together under difficult circumstances. But in the end, they go their separate ways. The benefit is that they learn to bond with whomever they are working with. The skill of bonding—of building oneness—is a transferrable skill.

Kronos speaks of a specific time.
Kyros speaks of an opportune time.
Horaios speaks of the right time.

When these three are properly aligned, you experience a dynamo release of *Dunamis*.

Building Oneness

In any group situation, the best thing to do is learn other people's strengths and weaknesses, then work to augment those qualities. This is why we teach redemptive gifting (sometimes called Motivational Gifting). It helps people understand themselves and others. From Romans 12, redemptive gifts fall into these categories:

- Prophecy
- Ministry
- Teaching
- Exhortation
- Giving
- Ruling
- Mercy

When we understand what motivates us, we're better equipped to understand why we think the way we do. We understand our personal temperament. Married couples, for example, find deeper places in their relationships when they understand the motivations of each partner.

When you learn someone's personality, you know which projects are right for them. If I need a breakthrough in something, I'm not going to ask someone who is melancholy. I'm going to find that choleric person who's an eternal optimist like me, and I'm going to say, "Hey, look, this ministry is not doing well. We started working downtown with the homeless people, but it's falling apart. I need a breakthrough or the city's going to run us off. What do you think about it?"

The right person with the right motivation gift will respond, "I can do that! I'm on it!"

I know that when I send them down there, they will bring it together. This is alignment in action.

Purpose of Alignment

Unity is built on encouragement. Oneness—becoming one—is built on purpose.

Churches often get together for community outreaches. They bring in the lost, the homeless, those seeking a spiritual home. They feed them, sing to them, maybe preach to them. It's a good thing to do; it encourages the hopeless. Yet we must understand the need to move beyond just being encouraged. We need to build on the purpose of the gathering. Getting together to feel good is a starting point, but without an end goal in mind, we are merely a social club.

I was once asked to join a meeting involving the reconciliation of two state leaders. The meeting organizers recognized me as an apostle, and they wanted me to participate in a preplanning session. At the start, however, they dove into a random discussion; it all seemed pointless to me. Finally, I spoke up.

"Wait. Let's set some boundaries here. Now, please understand: boundaries are not limitations. Boundaries keep us on track. They get us to our destination."

The shock of the organizers was palatable.

"What do you mean, Clay?"

"What's the purpose of this meeting?" I asked. "What's the expected outcome?"

"Well, um…the purpose is for the two state leaders in question to be reconciled," they said.

"And the expected outcome is that we never have to speak about this again?" I asked.

"Yes, that's right," they assured me.

"Well...." I said. "I recently worked with these same two leaders in a dynamic, state-wide meeting, and they're working great together."

In anything you do, there needs to be a purpose; there needs to be an expected outcome. And sometimes, through the exercise of identifying the purpose, you discover that it's not what you thought it was at all.

Unity Diluted Oneness

Unity releases a temporary momentum. Oneness creates synergy that maximizes the purpose.

I realize that unity is in the Bible. Psalm 133:1 tells us:

Behold, how good and how pleasant it is
For brothers to live together in unity!

Paul says in Ephesians 4:

Being diligent to keep the unity of the Spirit in the bond of peace (v. 3)

Until we all attain to the unity of the faith, (v. 13)

In Colossians 3:14, we read:

In addition to all these things put on love, which is the perfect bond of unity.

What all these verses have in common is that they were written a long time ago; the unity they were talking about is different than what people mean today. In many places, well-meaning ministers of various faiths and denominations get together for "Unity Meetings." It is so prevalent that it has a name: the Unity Movement. And that's great, as far as movements go. They are seeking peace. Whenever people of varying convictions and perspectives can share views together without a fistfight, I have to call that progress. The weakness of these efforts, however, is their tendency to devolve to the lowest common denominator—usually, the weakest denominator.

Praying in the spirit bothers you? We'll stop doing that.

Prophecy bothers you? We'll forget about it.

Don't believe in prophecy? It's gone…outta here…zip.

Authority of scripture? Oh well…we never believed it anyway.

In the end, we have a unified organization at the expense of the integrity of scripture and the experience of Holy Spirit. This kind of unity cannot bring about the Kingdom of God. We need the oneness that unites us in God, not in man.

Jesus said:

Do not think that I came to bring peace on the earth; I did not come to bring peace, but a sword.

Matthew 10:34

Certainly, this can be taken out of context. We are not called to arm ourselves and join a militia in the name of Jesus. Still, the guy who challenged the ruling Jewish elite with invectives such as: "scribes, Pharisees, hypocrites!" was never one to shrink from a fight. Turmoil is a fact of life. This is why Jesus promised his disciples:

These things I have spoken to you so that in Me you may have peace. In the world you have tribulation, but take courage; I have overcome the world.

John 16:33

True peace is realized by working through turmoil, not avoiding it. What good is the peace of unity if we bleach out the power of God? A move of God challenges the status quo; it upsets "normal." If we rule out anything that causes people to feel agitated, triggered or unsafe, we

Unity and Oneness

will negate God's intervention in the world's systems. We are not here to placate evil or the systems which compromise with evil. We are here as a part of a move of God, and sometimes, that gets rough.

9

Aligned Through Commissioning

IN MATTHEW 22:14, we have a famous quote of Jesus: "Many are called but few are chosen." What is less well-known is that, in the original Greek, it really says, "Many are called but a few <u>choose to be chosen</u>." That's a totally different statement. Many Christians today are not choosing to be chosen for ministry. Some are reluctant to get involved. Others doubt their God-given abilities. And still others, tragically, are waiting for an invitation that will never come…because it's already been given. It came in the form of opportunity.

The prophet Isaiah experienced it this way:

Then I heard the voice of the Lord, saying, "Whom shall I send, and who will go for Us?" Then I said, "Here am I. Send me!"

Isaiah 6:8

God did not command Isaiah; instead, he involved Isaiah in the decision-making process and Isaiah responded.

There was a man named C.C. Ford, who was a major builder and developer in Denver. He made millions of dollars and then moved to Tulsa where he started building houses there and made millions more. He met Demos Shakarian, the National leader and founder of the Full Gospel Businessmen movement. He was so impacted by Demos and his ministry that he volunteered to become Demos' pilot and flew him all across America helping him hold meetings.

C.C. Ford and his son purchased land in northwest Arkansas. Jim Lovell bought part of it from him, and we bought it from the Lovells. CC Ford bought tens of thousands of acres in northwest Arkansas for around $200/acre. Many years later, it fetched $3,000/acre.

C. C. Ford chose to be chosen, and not only was he rewarded for it, but his actions led directly to our obtaining the Ark property. He saw a need, stepped forward, answered a call and fit in perfectly to God's plan.

*****

Jim Lovell was a Professor and Department Head of Veterinary Medicine at the University of Illinois. By attending a Full Gospel Businessmen with Demos Shakarian and C.C. Ford, where Ford was telling people that he had some land in Arkansas that he wanted to sell, Jim said he was interested. There, at that meeting, he was introduced to Christ and his life was changed forever. Along with his first wife, Ann, they saw the opportunity to purchase the land in Arkansas and made a major change in their lives smuggling Bibles behind the Iron Curtain.

He resigned his position and set about doing what he felt God wanted him to do. He was never told specifically which opportunity to take. He didn't need that. He was primed and motivated, and he moved on the opportunity. He could have stayed in his comfortable post as a tweed-jacketed college professor. Instead, he chose to be chosen.

Part of the land that Jim Lovell purchased in northwest Arkansas was joined by property that Jim & Gwin Shaw also purchased from

C.C. Ford. That whole valley that they purchased became the world headquarters for The End-Time Handmaidens. What a divine connection!

Another part of land purchased by the Lovells was north of Harrison, Arkansas where they built a house and named the property, The Ark. Jim's wife, Ann, passed away from illness, later met Francine who was working with Gwen Shaw and The End-Time Handmaidens. Francine traveled worldwide with Gwen as a translator as she was born in France and was able to translate in many French-speaking countries.

Jim and Francine married and continued ministry from The Ark. After being married for around 25 years, Jim passed away and God used Francine to introduce us to The Ark. She was insistent that God wanted the land to come to us so she made us a deal that we couldn't refuse. So here we are!

Just look at all the opportunities that were available and acted upon in this series of events and actions that led to our acquiring the ministry center God had for us. Amazing what God can do, more than we could ever think of or make happen ourselves.

*****

Francine Lovell's husband, Jim Lovell, received a prophecy: "You're going to become a Bible smuggler into China."

Soon afterward, Jim, who had tenure at a college in Illinois, saw an opportunity to smuggle Bibles into China and decided to pursue it. He resigned his position and set about doing what he felt God wanted him to do. He was never told specifically which opportunity to take. He didn't need that. He was primed and motivated, and he moved on the opportunity. He could have stayed in his comfortable post as a tweed-jacketed college professor. Instead, he chose to be chosen.

Not everything we do in our spiritual journey is going to be micromanaged by God. Not everything that pleases God is dictated. When Jesus healed ten lepers, he gave them specific instructions:

And as He entered a village, ten men with leprosy who stood at a distance met Him; and they raised their voices, saying, "Jesus, Master, have mercy on us!" When He saw them, He said to them, "Go and show yourselves to the priests." And as they were going, they were cleansed.

Luke 17:12-14

The lepers did exactly what Jesus told them to do, and they were cleansed. That much was good. But look at what happened next:

Now one of them, when he saw that he had been healed, turned back, glorifying God with a loud voice, and he fell on his face at His feet, giving thanks to Him. And he was a Samaritan.

But Jesus responded and said, "Were there not ten cleansed? But the nine—where are they? Was no one found who returned to give glory to God, except this foreigner?"

And He said to him, "Stand up and go; your faith has made you well."

(vs. 15-19)

Jesus wondered where the other nine were. Well…they were doing what they had been told to do, right? Jesus never said: "When you are cleansed, come back and give glory to God." Yet he clearly was pleased when it happened. The Samaritan was not commanded to give glory to God. Instead, he chose to give glory to God.

God is looking for people who choose to be chosen.

In the NASB, the scripture reads:

You did not choose Me but I chose you, and <u>appointed you</u> that you would go and bear fruit, and that your fruit would remain, so that whatever you ask of the Father in My name He may give to you.

John 15:16

That phrase *appointed you* can be translated as "ordained you" or "commissioned you." Our confidence should be in our appointment. We are appointed by God to do his will. It's a given. So, as important as it is to know God's will and timing, we might not always have detailed instructions. It might be simply: "Go…and do." Expecting something more, we can easily succumb to "the paralysis of analysis." We can be dialed in so deeply to the details of walking in the spirit that we miss the big picture. Instead of waiting for an audible voice of God, we should look to a simpler direction: *There is a need; you have a skill; go for it.* This is what is meant by: "chose to be chosen." And trust God that he will lead you.

Further in this chapter, we are going to look at the three commissions of David. As we do, will we see a pattern. David continually chose to be chosen. He volunteered to fight Goliath. There is no record of God telling David to confront the giant. No conversation with a burning bush. No call to step out of the boat and walk across the water. There is nothing wrong with things like this; they are a part of our godly experience. However, they are not the only way God leads us. We can…and *should*…step out based on opportunity.

David knew Goliath needed slaying, and he was confident he could do it. He didn't think: *I am the man appointed by God for this task.* No, he thought: *it needs done, and I can do it.*

David jumped into the fray and fought the good fight. And he did it all from a place of submission to the Father.

Commissioning

When we commission people, we often find they are already functioning in their assignment. Therefore, our commission is a recognition of the alignment already in their hearts. Commissioning calls forth a synergy to be released through the power of agreement.

God said to Moses, "Take Joshua the son of Nun—the Spirit is in him!—and place your hand on him. Stand him before

> *Eleazar the priest in front of the entire congregation and commission him with everyone watching. Pass your magisterial authority over to him so that the whole congregation of the People of Israel will listen obediently to him. He is to consult with Eleazar the priest who, using the oracle-Urim, will prayerfully advise him in the presence of God. He will command the People of Israel, the entire community, in all their comings and goings."*
>
> Numbers 27:19-21 MSG

Moses told the people to select people for commissioning from among their ranks. He specified wise, understanding and seasoned individuals. He told them to find leaders—people already functioning in leadership—so he could commission them as leaders.

> *Select some wise, understanding, and seasoned men from your tribes, and I will commission them as your leaders.*
>
> Deuteronomy 1:13 MSG

Of course, today we would say, "Select some wise, understanding, and seasoned men *and women* from your tribes, and I will commission them as your leaders." In our modern times, we recognize that "there is neither Jew nor Greek, there is neither slave nor free, there is neither male nor female; for you are all one in Christ Jesus" (Galatians 3:28).

We find the same call to commissioning in Joshua:

> *Pick three men from each tribe so I can commission them. They will survey and map the land, showing the inheritance due each tribe, and report back to me.*
>
> Joshua 18:4 MSG

By laying out their task: "survey and map the land," Joshua specified the qualifications of those to be selected. He did not expect the search team to return with a gaggle of men and say, "Hey Josh, here you go. These screwballs don't know a map from a sheep's butt. They've never surveyed anything more than the buffet at Denny's. But we are offering them up in faith, that whom God calls, he qualifies."

No, that's not how it works. Because our calling is deep within our DNA, we will find ourselves doing the very thing God is calling us to do but on a greater level. Many people do the will of God simply by doing what seems natural. Do we need to commission mothers to nurse their infants? Do we need to commission fathers to provide for their families? No…but we do need to commission those same people to oversee outreaches for single mothers or to lead men's groups that teach parental responsibility.

Commissioning calls us into alignment for a greater work of God. It takes us from our calling ("many are called") to being sent forth ("few are chosen"). We don't need alignment to feed a child; we do need alignment to run a kitchen for homeless people. Commissioning brings us the resources to do a greater work than what we can do alone. It also aligns us with God's heart for a particular ministry. Just as we find ourselves doing naturally what God is calling us to, we find God at work preparing the situation for our eventual participation.

A spiritual son of ours, Dwayne, took a team to every county seat in Arkansas and conducted worship there. There are seventy-five counties in the State of Arkansas, and there are eighty-five county seats. (Some of our counties have dual county seats because of the way the county is made.) Dwayne took a discovery team to each courthouse and had many spiritual encounters. In one courthouse, they met a group who were expecting them.

"You're the ones, aren't you?" said a woman.

"What do you mean?" asked Dwayne.

"The Lord told us somebody from him was coming here today."

"The Lord woke me up last night," said a man. "He said, 'Come here. Be at this courthouse today.' And so, we are! Now you're here."

When you move out to do things God's way, you find he has already been there before you arrive. He's already working. It's his divine providence.

We find commissioning in the New Testament as well, and for things other than ministry.

> *One day as they were worshiping God—they were also fasting as they waited for guidance—the Holy Spirit spoke: "Take Barnabas and Saul and commission them for the work I have called them to do."*
>
> Acts 13:2 MSG

"The work I have called them to do," means anything God has called you to; this doesn't necessarily mean ministry. In our community, if you're going to start a business, go to college, buy a house, or sell a house—anything major—we commission you to do it. Commissioning conveys the power of agreement through alignment. The difference is that you are now *sent* to do something, not merely *called* to do something.

"For where two or three have gathered together in My name, I am there in their midst" (Matthew 18:20). When two or three people come together and agree on earth, that's being aligned. God is found wherever there's alignment.

A lot of people try to build ministries because they have a call of God upon their lives to do so, but they have never been commissioned and sent apostolically to do it. To be sent, you need a place to be sent from; you must be aligned to be sent. This is how the power flows to accomplish what you are called to do. It is the power of agreement.

> *I say to you that if two of you agree on earth concerning anything that they ask, it will be done for them by My Father in heaven. For where two or three are gathered together in My name, I am there in the midst of them.*
>
> Matthew 18:19-20 NKJV

Faithful in All Things

Moreover, it is required in stewards that they be found faithful.
1 Corinthians 4:2

Commissioning is facilitated through alignment; this involves being faithful in all things—even the little things.

Years ago, we ran classes for sons and daughters. It was a tough school. I insisted that they attend faithfully. I told them: "You don't call in sick. You *crawl* in sick. If you miss two classes in a year, you are out of the class. You can start over next year."

Remarkably, I only lost one student during the seven years we conducted these classes. I brought them to the place of understanding of how to be faithful, and they honored that requirement.

One Saturday, I showed up for class and I said, "Everybody go out and unlock your car."

Now, they were all young people; they worked hard but were not financially well off. Many struggled in life as well.

I looked inside everyone's car. I found empty Coke cans, fast food bags, trash, tools, and dirt. Some cars smelled like coffee…or worse. I said, "You're not being faithful in little things. Y'all want a better car?"

"Yes," they answered. "We need better cars."

"Then you have to be faithful with the one you have. Treat your car like a Lamborghini, and God will bless you with something greater. That's being faithful."

When I consider coming into alignment with people, I look for those who are faithful in little things. Only then do I know they will be faithful in greater things.

Everybody wants to be faithful with the greater things, the fancy things, but we tend to neglect the plain, ordinary things. When Jacob contended with Laban for his wives, he wanted Rachel, who was attractive, but instead, he was given Leah, who is described as being weak in her eyes. People today want the stunning spouse, the majestic house, the flashy car, the prestigious job. It's interesting, however, that the lineage of Jesus comes through Jacob and Leah, not Jacob and Rachel. According to Jewish history, Leah faithfully prayed for Rachel to have a child. In fact, she nearly fasted herself to death during her time of intercession.

We need to be faithful like Leah. Beauty is only skin deep. The commonplace of ministry is where the strength lies: cleaning carpets, driving an old van, making coffee, staying late to turn off lights. The figurehead of a ship is what everyone sees. But it's the ship's keel—the unsung foundation of the hull, out of sight below the waterline—that bears the load. Being faithful in small things, the seemingly insignificant things, is being faithful in the things that really matter, and that leads us to commissioning. Besides, the figurehead is only attractive until the paint starts peeling.

David's First Commission

King David, the man God used to replace Saul as the King of Israel, experienced three commissions. Together, they were a progression to gradually bring him into alignment with key individuals and organizations until he was positioned to assume the throne of Israel.

> *Now the Lord said to Samuel, "How long are you going to mourn for Saul, since I have rejected him from being king over Israel? Fill your horn with oil and go; I will send you to Jesse the Bethlehemite, because I have chosen a king for Myself among his sons."*
>
> 1 Samuel 16:1

Samuel knew he'd been sent by God, but he was looking for a tall, good-looking man like Saul: the last king he'd commissioned. But God had other ideas.

Aligned Through Commissioning

When they entered, he looked at Eliab and thought, "Surely the Lord's anointed is standing before Him." But the Lord said to Samuel, "Do not look at his appearance or at the height of his stature, because I have rejected him; for God does not see as man sees, since man looks at the outward appearance, but the Lord looks at the heart."

1 Samuel 16:6-7

After reviewing and rejecting each of Jesse's sons, David was requested to come out of the field and, to the astonishment of all, was commissioned among his brothers and the townspeople of Bethlehem.

So Samuel took the horn of oil and anointed him in the midst of his brothers; and the Spirit of the Lord rushed upon David from that day forward.

1 Samuel 16:13

David's first commissioning was conducted in the midst of his family. He wasn't even present when Samuel requested that Jesse and his sons attend the sacrifice in Bethlehem. He was in the pasture faithfully looking after the sheep, and he continued doing so after his commissioning.

Have you ever asked yourself why the youngest in the family was looking after the sheep when the rest of the family responded to the most feared prophet in all the land? It was because David was an illegitimate child of Jesse. As such, he was insignificant; possibly a source of shame.

Why was David commissioned in the midst of his brothers? Because who knows you better than your family? His brothers knew his ups and downs. His brothers knew if he had ever told a lie. His brothers watched him grow up: cutting teeth, potty training, learning to ride a chariot without training wheels. He was the little brother that everyone overlooked…until the Spirit of the Lord came upon him.

Tending sheep was a lowly job—an unglamorous but necessary task that carries no prestige. But David was faithful in this assignment, submitted to the authority of his father, and he would eventually be elevated because of it. Indeed, it was his training ground. It is interesting that after David's commissioning, he continued tending the sheep. We don't know how much time transpired until David stood before King Saul, but notice that Saul sought a musician for the palace band, David was described thusly by Saul's servant:

> *Behold, I have seen a son of Jesse the Bethlehemite who is a skillful musician, a valiant mighty man, a warrior, skillful in speech, and a handsome man; and the Lord is with him.*
> 1 Samuel 16:18

It appears that a development of sorts occurred after David's anointing. Why else did God send Samuel? The Spirit of the Lord came upon David, and he grew in strength. We know he killed a lion and a bear to protect the family flock; most likely, this occurred after the anointing.

See, David's first commissioning was to align him with God. David was positioned as the future king, but nobody on earth except Samuel even cared. He was still tending sheep—out of sight, out of mind. His brothers continued to abuse him. When he brought food to them as they hunkered down on the battlelines, afraid of Goliath, they were rather curt:

> *Now Eliab his oldest brother heard him when he spoke to the men; and Eliab's anger burned against David and he said, "Why is it that you have come down? And with whom have you left those few sheep in the wilderness? I myself know your insolence and the wickedness of your heart; for you have come down in order to see the battle."*
>
> *But David said, "What have I done now? Was it not just a question?" Then he turned away from him to another and said the same thing; and the people replied with the same words as before.*
> 1 Samuel 17:28-30

Aligned Through Commissioning

Wicked? Insolent? Is that any way to speak to the future king of Israel? Of course not. Yet Eliab did not know of David's destiny. He still saw David as the punk kid who stunk of sheep manure.

"What have I done now?" It was an insightful question. What David had done was to grow up. Aligned with the Spirit of God, he grew to be a mighty warrior who could carry a tune and pluck a mean harp. He was being prepared for his destiny. Notice that he was no longer merely aligned with his brothers. The commissioning by Samuel had ushered in a greater alignment. Still, he had to remain faithful to the things God was using to develop him.

It was his experience protecting the family flock that convinced Saul to let him have a go with Goliath.

> *Saul said to David, "You are not able to go against this Philistine to fight him; for you are only a youth, while he has been a warrior since his youth."*
>
> *But David said to Saul, "Your servant was tending his father's sheep. When a lion or a bear came and took a sheep from the flock, I went out after it and attacked it, and rescued the sheep from its mouth; and when it rose up against me, I grabbed it by its mane and struck it and killed it. Your servant has killed both the lion and the bear; and this uncircumcised Philistine will be like one of them, since he has defied the armies of the living God."*
>
> 1 Samuel 17:33-36

Of course, we all know the results. David came out ahead in his contest with Goliath, and his victory would be celebrated for generations. But notice: nobody praised him when he was a shepherd boy. Nobody sang, "David killed that bear! He killed that lion. Yay, David!" No, that must have missed everyone's attention…everyone except God.

Alignment with God often escapes the notice of others. No matter. We don't align for the praise of men. David's first alignment was with God, and in this, he was faithful.

Imagine how things would have gone if David had not been faithful in the small things, (as if killing a lion was small). Imagine his conversation with Saul going like this:

Saul said to David, "You are not able to go against this Philistine to fight him; for you are only a youth, while he has been a warrior since his youth."

But David said to Saul, "Your servant was tending his father's sheep...when he wasn't sleeping off his wine or chasing shepherdesses from other pastures.

When a lion or a bear came and took a sheep from the flock, I ran. Who wants to fight something with claws a cubit long?

So yeah...about this uncircumcised Philistine, here's the deal. I'll stride forth, call his momma a bunch of names, and run. When he chases me, I'll jump over the rocks where the army is hiding. They'll knock the stuffing out of him, and I'll get all the credit.

How's that sound...King?"

1 Clay 17:33-36

In churches today, we confuse calling with commissioning through alignment. Let's say we've got this great prophetic gifting and we show up at a church service. We assume the leader is so discerning that she's going to see our prophet mantle, put us up front, and set us to prophesying.

Well, that's not what's going to happen. A mantle is not everything. Character is everything. Faithfulness is everything. Trustworthiness is everything. These qualities are established through alignment. If you care enough to minister in our meetings, then you should care enough to align with our ministry. We are shepherds tending a flock, and we do it zealously. Bears and lions need not apply. David was faithful in his alignment with his family. Later, after Samuel anointed him, he was faithful in his alignment with God.

Many people struggle with this concept.

In our church in Dyersburg, we were conducting Sunday night services geared around the prophetic. One night, a man in the back row stood up and declared: "I've been coming here for six Sunday nights. I've driven an hour and a half each way, and you've not yet recognized me as a prophet."

I said to my deacon, "Help him find the door."

The man did not come to receive from a prophet; he came to be recognized as a prophet. As a result, he was recognized for what he really was, and we never saw him again.

David wasn't down in the pasture so he could be recognized. He was down there being faithful...aligned and faithful.

David's Second Commission

Then it came about afterward that David inquired of the Lord, saying, "Shall I go up to one of the cities of Judah?"

And the Lord said to him, "Go up."

So David said, "Where shall I go up?"

And He said, "To Hebron."

So David went up there, and his two wives also, Ahinoam the Jezreelitess and Abigail the widow of Nabal the Carmelite. And David brought up his men who were with him, each with his household; and they settled in the cities of Hebron. Then the men of Judah came, and there they anointed David king over the house of Judah.

2 Samuel 2:1-4

Saul was dead, Saul's son Jonathan was also dead, and Israel was without a king. David's first commission aligned him with God. His second commission aligned him with a specific delegation as king over the house of Judah. He still operated under another man's authority; Judah was included in the leadership of Israel.

As an example, a US senator from Texas is part of the leadership of the United States of America. He is not the leader of the country; he is a specific delegation. He represents the people of Texas, but decisions are made in Washington, DC. The senator is part of that decision-making process.

When David was delegated to be the king of the tribe of Judah, he was included in the leadership of Israel, and his development as the future King of Israel continued. He remained faithful.

Today, when the leadership in a church asks you to do something—whether it's being the soundman or stocking the restroom, you're included in the leadership. Your function might not be to sit with the elders when they're deciding what the will of God is in a certain area, but you're included in leadership as far as your responsibility goes. The soundperson sets the speakers and amplifiers. The maintenance person decides when to change the air filters. The janitor decides between Charmin or Wal-Mart toilet paper. The groundskeeper determines when to mow the grass.

Alignment with leadership takes many forms.

David's Third Commission

David's third and final commissioning came from the elders of Israel, not just those of Judah.

> *Then all the tribes of Israel came to David at Hebron and spoke, saying, "Indeed we are your bone and your flesh. Also, in time past, when Saul was king over us, you were the one who led Israel out and brought them in; and the Lord*

said to you, 'You shall shepherd My people Israel, and be ruler over Israel.'"

Therefore all the elders of Israel came to the king at Hebron, and King David made a covenant with them at Hebron before the Lord. And they anointed David king over Israel. David was thirty years old when he began to reign, and he reigned forty years.

2 Samuel 5:1-4

At thirty years old, David was now commissioned over Israel. David was commissioned over Israel because he had been faithful with Judah. He was now aligned with the people: "We are your bone and your flesh." He had been tried, tested and made worthy. The people had determined to trust him, and he had earned their respect.

David's journey was a process of relational alignment, gradually becoming fitly joined together with others, accepting their supply and giving of his supply.

10

Authority and Leadership

EFFECTIVE LEADERSHIP MUST BE BASED on relational authority, and that flows through alignment. When I align with those under me—people serving in areas over which I have responsibility—I am a leader. When I align with those over me—people whose God-given task is to keep me between the navigational buoys—they are the leaders.

The flow of authority has nothing to do with who is better than who; how would we even begin to determine that? Authority flows according to responsibility. Where has God placed you? What has he assigned you to do?

Alignment for conquest has nothing to do with top-down power structures. Marriage is for conquest, but it does not set one person over the other. It sets both people under God, indivisible, with liberty and justice for all. Likewise, alignment in the church is not done so that a certain class of people is seen as leaders and others are understood to be underlings. This unfortunate model dates back centuries, to the separation of clergy and laity. From the Catholic Encyclopedia:

> The laity and clergy, or clerics, belong to the same society, but do not occupy the same rank. The laity are the members

of this society who remain where they were placed by baptism, while the clergy, even if only tonsured, have been raised by ordination to a higher class, and placed in the sacred hierarchy.

In the early centuries of the fledgling church, the clergy were the only people who could read. The laity was considered foolish, ignorant, and (most importantly) *unable* to learn. As the educated gathered power over the unlearned, the separation grew. Pulpits rose higher and the chasm grew deeper.

> *Effective leadership must be based on relational authority, and that flows through alignment.*

True alignment can't happen in a "command and control" paradigm. Many systems of man work that way, to the detriment of all involved. When we build a church structure based on hierarchy, it actually deprives the people of power. No longer free to seek God and develop their giftings, the driving motivation becomes "What does the leader want?"

In our church, we have revised our membership model. People are considered shareholders; they are known for their areas of responsibility, and everyone respects each other's areas. I don't touch the sound system. I don't interfere with the intercessors (though I might join them). I revel in the fresh revelations coming out of our teachers. In the truest sense of Ephesians 4, we are aligning the saints for the works of ministry. The key is this: establish teachers and let them teach; establish evangelists and let them evangelize; establish shepherds and let them shepherd; establish the prophets and get ready—stuff's fixin' to get real.

When David was first commissioned, he was aligned horizontally. He was not appointed above this family. He was still the shepherd boy; still the snot-nosed little brother; still facing his challenges in the sheep pastures. He was discovering, growing and being prepared for leadership. He learned a lot, and he did so because he was aligned horizontally with his family and aligned vertically with God.

Iron On Iron

A lot of people seek alignment because they want camaraderie, and that's fine, as far as it goes. We all need to find our tribe. We need to discover our DNA. We need to learn where we fit, because there is where we find life. However, we also need to get around people who are not our type so we can be challenged, even enlightened, on things we haven't thought of. "As iron sharpens iron, so one person sharpens another" (Proverbs 27:17). One of the great pleasures in life is to discover that you don't know all you thought you knew. It's called learning.

About twenty years ago, I went through a process of asking myself why I believed everything I believed. I took all the fundamentals, the basics, and challenged them. *Why do I believe this? Why do I think that?* I discovered the reason I believed some things was because someone I admired taught it, so I adapted it and brought it into my belief system. In my introspection, I realized that my belief system was based more on favorable impressions than it was God's truth. I needed to pursue truth.

In praying for his disciples on the eve of the crucifixion, Jesus asked the father to "Sanctify them in the truth." Then he qualified it: "Your word is truth" (John 17:17).

God's word is truth. Not necessarily all that we interpret from the Bible—we can be easily misled—but what God breathes through those holy words, passing our misconceptions and entering our hungry souls. Think about that for a moment. When you are with someone, when do you feel their breath? It's when you are closest to them, right? So, if you want the God-breathed truth, draw near to him. This is alignment; this is sharing of spirit to spirit. Only by aligning with truth do we become one with truth. When God speaks, faith arises and we believe. His word is truth.

When God began giving us words saying we were to acquire land in Arkansas, and that one day we would establish a healing and training center, we began to believe it. As God continued speaking to us about acquiring land, faith came to us, and through faith, things which did not yet exist became real.

> *(as it is written: "I have made you a father of many nations") in the presence of Him whom he believed, that is, God, who gives life to the dead and calls into being things that do not exist.*
>
> Romans 4:17

When we came into faith, we aligned with the truth that God had given to us; we became one with that truth. When you become one with something, you move beyond just *believing* it. Now you *know* it. It's in the knowing that we conceive, as the venerable King James told us. "Adam knew his wife; and she conceived" (Genesis 4:1).

Today, I know Jesus was crucified, buried and resurrected. I don't know it because I read it in a book. And no, I wasn't here (despite what my Grandkids think). I know it because God has breathed on what is written in the Bible, and I have become one with that. I have become aligned with God's truth.

Through alignment, we can do far greater things than we could even imagine while working alone.

> *That in the dispensation of the fullness of the times He might gather together in one all things in Christ, both which are in heaven and which are on earth—in Him.*
>
> Ephesians 1:10

Consider the word *dispensation*. Another word that could be translated in its place is *stewardship*. The words *dispensation* and *stewardship* are really the same word. It is Strong's NT #346 *anakephalaioó*. It means, "to briefly comprehend or gather together in one."

When you come into alignment, you are gathered together in one new man. In the process, you lose your individuality of identity, but you gain a greater identity. God wants to bring us into alignment where the value of each of us together is a greater value.

What we are alone is not nearly as much as what we can be together. There is a synergic release when people fitly join together. Only through alignment do we get the synergic release of the sum total of the value of all of us.

Have you ever worked on a team? I used to run a kingdom think tank, and anybody could participate. To simulate creativity, I would bless the person who came up with the craziest idea with a gift card. Now, I wasn't looking for crazy ideas. I was looking to remove all boundaries, to where they were willing to put forth a crazy idea. It worked. In fact, it worked too well. We had more crazy ideas than we had crazy people to implement them.

The key was keeping people from feeling intimidated. All it takes is someone thinking outside of the box for something to be improved. When we come together, we bring value, we challenge each other, we bring out the best in each other.

Unity is the beginning of the power of agreement. If I say to someone with an idea, "I want to come into agreement with you," I'm beginning the process. We're unified now because we've chosen to come in agreement. But we have to journey until we come to completed faith; before we are really in agreement. Unity means you have a seat on the train. But the train is still sitting in the station. The destination is elsewhere; it's the journey that gets us there.

God created and designed us. When we come into alignment, we bring the strength we have, and we also bring our weaknesses. We are people, after all. The good news is, the strength of others offsets our weaknesses. When alignment is authentic, our weaknesses are compensated for, even as our strengths are required for another's weaknesses.

Anyone married for any length of time understands this. Married people complement each other. They have to. It's the only way they survive, much less flourish. Now, personally, I don't believe there was only one woman in the world that God designed for me to marry. I married Susan Riffey. Her family is German. However, I do believe there was one *type* of woman who would complement and complete me.

When we get legalistic, we miss God's truth. There is a false teaching about God's will, one that divides it into an acceptable will and a perfect will. In marriage, as in alignment, we don't align with perfect people. We align with people with whom we are compatible; people with whom we can come into unity. We align with people who will get on the train and take the journey with us. Perfection comes as we learn to work together, as we uncover our strengths and weaknesses and figure out how they fit jointly together. A perfect marriage—indeed, a perfect relationship—is made, not discerned. God's perfect will is that we work our tails off and make alignment work. They shall *become* one (ref. Genesis 2:24).

Ephesians 1:10 is about the one new man.

regarding His plan of the fullness of the times, <u>to bring all things together in Christ</u>, things in the heavens and things on the earth.

Ephesians 4:11-12 tells us how.

And He gave some as apostles, some as prophets, some as evangelists, some as pastors and teachers, for the equipping of the saints for the work of ministry, for the building up of the body of Christ;

"For the *katartizō* of the saints." Expanded: "the equipping, perfecting, maturing of the saints." This is the actual word *aligning*; Paul is saying: "for the aligning of the saints."

Leadership

For alignment to work, we have to trust people: the leaders before us, the co-workers beside us, and the supporters behind us. Trust is a choice. We *choose* to trust someone. After we trust them, they have the opportunity to earn our respect. Trust brings us into unity. Respect is developed on the journey.

I like to ask people: what's the population on planet Earth? I get a variety of answers, usually in the billions. Smiling, I tell them: "You missed it by a little. The population of planet Earth is two—those who are in Christ and those who are in Adam."

Yes, we're all individuals, but God's goal is to see the one new man standing up on the earth today. Jesus is not the second Adam; he's the last Adam. That's what scripture says. We are either in Christ or in Adam. We are either gathered together in Christ—sharing in the blood covenant and all the blessings it conveys—or we are still in Adam.

This is what Hebrews 10:5 describes:

> *You have not desired sacrifice and offering,*
> *But You have prepared a body for Me.*

John wrote about this, and although he appears to be describing the return of Christ, isn't that presence our goal in everything we do? When we come into alignment, the end goal is to "be like him," to "see him just as he is."

> *Beloved, now we are children of God, and it has not appeared as yet what we will be. We know that <u>when He appears, we will be like Him</u>, because <u>we will see Him just as He is.</u>*
>
> 1 John 3:2

He's bringing us together. But it's not always easy. This is not a gaggle of random strangers joining hands and singing Kum Ba Yah. Becoming fitly joined together takes work. The journey is difficult at times, and it doesn't always go as we thought it would…or should.

For example, many churches have prophetic teams, and everybody wants to be on the prophetic team. Everybody wants to be a prophet. And why not? You get to stand up at the front, looking tall and mighty, and read other people's mail. And the best part? Nobody gets to read their mail. (Or so they think.)

The part people don't see, however, is the hardship behind it. Most people have no idea the homework it takes to be on a prophetic team. Nothing is free. The failure of an assignment, or a ministry, or a marriage is NOT because you missed the perfect will of God. Remember, the perfect will of God is that we align (unity) and work hard together (journey) to attain the presence of Christ (oneness) in the God-given area of focus.

It's not the demons that are opposing us. It's a little closer to home. Paul, who wrote two-thirds of the New Testament, said in Romans 7:19,

For the good that I want, I do not do, but I practice the very evil that I do not want.

We have found the enemy, and he is us. I find that I wrestle with my flesh—that part of me that is still undergoing redemption—far greater than I do demons.

Strongs NT #346 *anakephalaioó*, is made up of the Strong's #303 *aná* and the Strong #2775 *kephalaióō*. In its original sense, it simply means, "to sum up."

Ephesians 2:5 NKJV says:

Even when we were dead in trespasses, made us alive together with Christ (by grace you have been saved).

The NASB puts it slightly differently:

Even when we were dead in our wrongdoings, made us <u>alive together</u> with Christ (by grace you have been saved).

This phrase *alive together* is from the Strong's NT word #4806 *suzoopoieo*. It's from the Strong's NT word #4862 *syn* and #2227 *zōopoiéō*. It means "to reanimate conjointly with." In other words, "to be quickened together." To be made *alive together* with Christ means, "to revive," or "to resuscitate." It means "to revive, to reset, and to restore to life even as a person who is dead or apparently dead, to reanimate a drowned person or to resuscitate."

We know the word *resuscitate* better than *reanimate*, but they're similar. *Reanimate* means "to restore to life or action, to conjoint, a united, connected, or even an associate." That sounds exactly like what happens in Christ.

In Union Together

Alignment is relational. It begins with a relational position related to our calling and moves into equipping. As discussed, there's a difference between being positioned for something and being equipped for something.

For example, I might ask Ruth: "We want you to pray about something. We want you to take over the prayer for this area."

That would position Ruth. However, once she prays about it and agrees, "I will do it," she assumes the responsibility, and with it, the empowerment.

Most people want greater authority—the authority to accomplish what God lays on their hearts. The way to greater authority is to be willing to take more responsibility. Back to my example, until Ruth agrees to the responsibility of leading prayer, she has no authority in that area. If she said, "No thank you, Clay. I'm too busy," she would have little power in that area. Only when she commits to the responsibility does she operate with authority.

I sometimes describe my personality this way: I will jump off a cliff and figure out how to make wings on the way down. I'm only partially joking. I've learned to answer God's call and move out, knowing the equipping will be there. It has taken me years to do this correctly. Most important is knowing that I have clearly heard from God. There is nothing wrong with a desire to do something; it's embedded in our God-given DNA. But to know when to go is a matter of being directed by God.

A friend of mine spent three days in prayer concerning his desire to work in Pakistan. He had the local contacts; he had the resources; he was a mature leader in overseas ministry. He had everything he needed…except the word of God. At the end of the three days, God said one word: "Go."

My friend launched his ministry and millions of Muslims have responded to the gospel. Yes…millions.

Authority is responsibility motivated by love.

One of the last things Jesus said to his disciples before he ascended is this:

All authority in heaven and on earth has been given to Me…
Matthew 28:18

Jesus could say this because he took responsibility for everything that was in heaven and earth. The atonement of the cross was motivated by love that encompassed the world:

For God so loved the world, that He gave His only Son, so that everyone who believes in Him will not perish, but have eternal life.

John 3:16

Authority and Leadership

It was love that led Jesus to the cross, and love that led him to receiving "all authority." Authority without love is slavery. Authority with love is alignment with the Father.

And raised us up together, and made us sit together in the heavenly places in Christ Jesus.

Ephesians 2:6 NKJV

Every time we read the word *together*, it is a different word in Greek. In Acts 19:15, where we read: "Jesus I know, and Paul I know; but who are you?" we find two different words for *know* in the Greek. Where it said, "Jesus, I know, and Paul, I know," what it actually says is, "Jesus, I know, and Paul, I'm *getting* to know."

The demons who inhabit the cosmos—the second heaven—were getting to know Paul. They knew him by his authority. In the spiritual realm around us, there are angels of light and angels of darkness. They coexist in that realm. We are also known there.

And raised us up together, and made us sit together in the heavenly places in Christ Jesus.

Ephesians 2:6 NKJV

Therefore, we must ask ourselves: What are we known for? Our authority can be faked before people; only authentic authority works in the spiritual realm.

A friend of mine was doing worship at an Aglow Christmas meeting in Greenville, Mississippi. The guest minister was ministering to people, and he stood in front of a man and said, "The Lord has shown me you have a lying demon."

The person shook his head and dropped his head in remorse. The guest minister said to him, "I'm going to take authority. In the name of Jesus, I cast you out."

The demon spoke to the minister and said, "You can't cast me out. You cheat on your income tax, and that's lying."

The meeting came to a halt.

You cannot have authority over anything in anybody else's life that you have not conquered in your own life.

Blessed be the God and Father of our Lord Jesus Christ, the Father of mercies and God of all comfort, who comforts us in all our tribulation, <u>that we may be able to comfort those who are in any trouble, with the comfort with which we ourselves are comforted by God.</u>

2 Corinthians 1:3-4

Only in the areas that you have conquered—the giants you've kicked off your mountain—do you have the authority to kick giants off other people's mountains. We can bind strongholds and cast out demons, but if we are not operating in true authority, those demonic forces can come back and attack us.

Vulnerability

Operating in the spirit leads us to vulnerability. Indeed, it requires it. Ministry is the ultimate revealing, both of all that is good within us and that which is still under construction. It is not long before we realize that the covering we thought hid us is actually a blindfold.

Look again at Ephesians 2:6:

And raised us up together, and made us sit together in the heavenly places in Christ Jesus.

The phrase "raised us up together" is from the Strong's NT # 4862 *sun*, and #1453 *egeiró*. It means, "to arouse from death in company with." In other words, "to revive spiritually." It also means, "to be raised up together, to rise with."

It's not really about resurrection, but it is about reviving. When people get close to death but don't die, they have to be revived and brought back. That's the sense of Ephesians 2:6.

Authority and Leadership

The phrase "made us sit together" is from a Strong's NT word #4776 *sugkathizó*. It's also like the previous word. It has a base in #4862 *sun*, but then also #2523 *kathizó*. It means "to give or take a seat in company with."

When Kings of old came together to make a covenant, they sat down together. They always carried their sword on their strong side. They would reach forth and lay their hand on the inner thigh of the other king. In so doing, they put themselves in a place of vulnerability.

See, Ephesians 2:6 is about more than just sitting side by side. It's about facing each other in a place of vulnerability. You will never be aligned until you're vulnerable. You will never build any depth of relational alignment without vulnerability.

When Susan and I married over 50 years ago (as of this writing), I had to make myself vulnerable. Would Susan stay with me? You all know my history for the first nine years; it was a challenge for her. I was a gambler. I was not saved. I was a workaholic. I was gone all the time. I loved good sipping whiskey. I bought it by the gallons. I'm serious. It was tough. We entered into our marriage covenant with a degree of vulnerability just like anybody does. We hoped for the best and we believed for the best.

Vulnerability does not mean you are aligning with a perfect person. Quite the opposite. In vulnerability, all our faults and weaknesses are exposed. They have to be. Exposure always reveals our strengths—both our developed strengths and our potential strengths. Exposure doesn't work like a filter. You can't broadcast your strengths and hide your failings. In fact, if you have to brag about your abilities, any discerning heart will realize you are also revealing your shortcomings. Vulnerability is all or nothing.

The key is knowing who you are choosing to align with. It doesn't mean being vulnerable with everyone. We're living in a time where you better walk with Holy Ghost.

Aligned for Conquest

> *Behold, I am sending you out as sheep in the midst of wolves;*
> *so be as wary as serpents, and as innocent as doves.*
> Matthew 10:16

I was in one of my favorite restaurants one evening, and I saw a man who bothered me. I didn't like the way he was carrying himself. Something was off; he seemed dangerous, so I watched him. As I prayed, the Lord said, "Don't ever become so comfortable in the places you're familiar with, that you don't stay on guard."

Now, the Lord was not advocating fear; he was instilling wisdom. I know the difference. I was raised in an atmosphere where I always sat with my back against the wall. We just need to be vulnerable when we choose to be. And we need to always be wise.

I knew a pilot, Lou Fields. He actually became a pastor. He flew for American Airlines out of Nashville. He was in Shoney's one day about two o'clock, having a cup of coffee, catching up on his paperwork before he flew to Nashville. Out of the corner of his eye, he saw two men enter with black masks over their faces. He didn't have a weapon, so he ducked under the table. They killed all four people in the restaurant. He survived. We need to be on our toes right now. Holy Spirit can give us an amber alert. Not fear, but wisdom.

When Susan and I minister to hardcore bikers, we love to see their lives change. When we associate with them, however, we carry ourselves carefully. We make sure we don't cross certain lines that could put us in danger. It's the same in any culture. When I'm in Ohio, I'm careful not to be seen adding sugar to my ice tea. You never know what will set off a fight with those folks above the Mason-Dixon line.

As I started to travel more and become busier, people called me all the time and said, "I'm going to get my pilot's license and start flying you to meetings."

"No, you're not," I'd say. "Until you have ten thousand hours, you're not flying me anywhere."

Why? Most of the small aircraft crashes are either mechanical (because the plane is not serviced properly), or the pilot is inexperienced. You need experience before I fly with you. I'll accept a measure of vulnerability, but I'm not stupid.

I did a Christian Bar Mitzvah (a rite of passage) for a boy, Ben, who turned thirteen. The church believes in the rite of passage into manhood. It was very interesting; I'd had an experience with the Lord in the midst of it.

The Lord told me that morning to give Ben a pocketknife for his rite of passage into manhood. "But don't you hand it to him closed or wrapped or in a package. You open it, and you hand him the handle."

I was always taught that if a man loaned you his pocket knife, you always handed it back to him open with the handle forward and the blade in your hand. The Lord explained where that custom comes from. It was a sign of trust and vulnerability. When you handed that man back his knife and he had the handle, he could easily use it on you. It actually was a sign of the covenant, a sign of trust and vulnerability.

What I didn't know at the time was that Ben collects pocket knives. It meant a lot to him.

Trust in Tithes and Offerings

Trust is a choice. Respect is earned. We'll never learn to respect someone until we first choose to trust them. Trust opens the door. People cannot earn our respect if we choose not to trust them. The reason people choose not to trust them is because of who we are. We all carry a past; we all have memories, experiences, wounds. The writer Anaïs Nin was right: "We don't see things as they are; we see things as we are."

Alignment requires that we share one another's values. Certainly, we will not align with every human being on earth. However, if we are trying to align with someone and it's just not happening, we need to look closer at what might be standing in the way.

In my ministerial life, a person cannot come into a relational covenant and alignment with me if they don't value tithing and the sowing of offerings. That's because Kingdom giving is a part of who I am—who God made me to be. It's more than collecting money; it's harnessing the power of seedtime and harvest). It's how we operate, how we get things done. It is God's profound service to mankind of unlocking the storehouses and pouring out a blessing we cannot contain.

Tithing is not ten percent; it's the first ten percent. In our church, we're running about 93% of the congregation tithing. Over 30% of the congregation match their tithes with ten percent offerings. That's the reason the vision is getting done, because people have partnered with us on that level. You can't be in relational covenant with me if you don't value the things I value.

I can say this because I live it. I practice what I expect from others. If you are unfamiliar or distrustful of tithing, you're going to be over cautious coming into that relational covenant with me. If you choose to trust me, however, you will see the benefits of tithes and offerings and your respect for me will be established. Our giving is to God, and it is God who promises to reward our giving. To see this, you must choose to trust him.

Another value of mine is authentic leadership.

When I first came to our church, a man told me, "I don't believe in the kind of church government you believe in."

"What do you believe in?" I asked.

"I believe in the plurality of eldership. I believe everybody's equal."

"You've read what happens in other churches that have tried that?"

"Yes."

"It didn't work out for them, did it?

"Well, that's how we did it in the church I came out of, and that's what I believe."

"Well," I said. "That's not happening here. If you can't serve in leadership because of that, I understand. But it's not happening."

Nine months later, he came back to me. "Look, I was wrong. Your style of leadership is far greater than the other leaders we've had in the past. And the reason is that you're a man of integrity."

He was talking about character integrity; I have accountability to other people. He knows that I am not a lone wolf. I'm not going off on my own agenda. I am in alignment with people over me, people beside me, and people under me. My authority—and the respect it engenders—flows from my alignment with others. It's the only way to function in the Kingdom of God.

Integrity Is About Being

In whom the whole building, being fitted together, grows into a holy temple in the Lord.

Ephesians 2:21

In Ephesians 2:21, the phrase "being fitted together, grows into a holy temple in the Lord," is from Strong's NT #4883 *sunarmologeó*. It also comes from #4862 *sun*. It's a derivative of the compound of Strong's #719 *harmos*, and #3004 *legó*. It's original sense means, "to render, close jointed together."

Think about tongue and groove hardwood flooring and how the pieces interlock together. They become integrated, fitly joined together. In this verse, it means, "to render close, jointed together, or to be organized or to be compacted, to be fitly framed or joined together." That is what God wants to do. The whole building must be fitted together to stand. This is a picture of integrity. It is not just us coming together in the room; it's about how we are fitly joined together. A truckload of lumber dumped on a worksite is not a building. Only when all the pieces are carefully installed can it stand.

We bought a Kroger store in Dyersburg, Tennessee and turned it into a church facility. It had all these support poles in the room because the trusses they used only spanned part of the way across the building. I got hold of an engineer I knew at the University of Arkansas, sending what I thought was the proper measurements of the trusses, so we could reinforce them and remove some of the poles to make the sanctuary easier to access. Well, we started into the job and discovered that the elder didn't measure the trusses correctly. The project turned into a fiasco, but we were able to eventually remove the poles.

It's the same way with the Body of Christ. You have to be properly fit in place. We have too many people trying to be positioned into a place they'll never be able to be postured for. While you can be positioned for nearly anything, being postured takes the grace of God, and that only comes through proper alignment.

Many people want to be on a prophetic team, but not everybody belongs on a prophetic team. Certainly, everybody is prophetic to some extent. They're prophetic because the prophetic is about hearing from God. If people are not hearing from God, what good is listening to a sermon or reading scripture. Unless it is God-breathed, it is not the Word of God. Everybody is prophetic, but everybody does not have the grace to be on a prophetic team. It's one thing to hear from God in prayer, during worship, and perhaps get a word for yourself or a neighbor. It's another thing to stand as a prophet and speak into people's lives in a life-changing way. To do that requires a specific grace, and for that, we must be built together.

In whom you also are being built together for a dwelling place of God in the Spirit.

Ephesians 2:22

In this passage, we move from being fitted together to being built together. This is Strong's NT word #4925, *sunoikodomeó*. It also ties into #4862 *sun*. It means "to construct," It is also "a composer of music, to compose." In the context of Christians being together, it means "to literally place or set together, to form a compound."

I occasionally work with a product called JB Weld. It comes in two parts: resin and hardener. When you mix it together, it forms a compound. There is a catalyst that brings the two ingredients together. Eventually, that compound hardens like steel.

In alignment, there has to be a catalyst to bring things together. It is called leadership honor.

Catalyst of Leadership Honor

Let me give you a definition of leadership.

A leader is someone that can take a group of people to a place they don't desire to go and cause them to discover that they have purpose and destiny there.

See, most people have never discovered their original design intent. If you choose to trust a good leader, he or she will earn your respect and get you properly positioned and postured for effectiveness in your life.

My son carries this so strongly. He amazes me. He has worked for a lawncare and landscaping business. While doing so, he said to the owner of the company, "I'll buy you a steak dinner if you'll do something on this job for me."

The owner was an Iraq war veteran, a great guy, driven and practical. He was intrigued. "What do you want me to do?"

"Let me be the boss today on the privacy fence job."

"What do you mean, *be the boss*?"

"How many days labor did you estimate for this job?"

Aligned for Conquest

"Four days."

"If you'll let me be the boss, I'll walk you out of here in fourteen hours—a single day."

"You can do that?"

"Yes, I can."

Well, the owner agreed and my son started leading.

"The first thing we have to address is the compressor: your compressor is not big enough. We are constantly waiting on it to build up air to run two air guns. Let's go to Home Depot and rent air guns that run on CO2. Then we're not tied to a hose and we will move faster working with that.

"The second thing is we are going to get out of bed in the morning at 5:30 instead of 8:30 like you normally do."

Well, they were on the job site at 7:00 AM. They finished up that day at about 9:00 PM. The job paid four days of labor, but it took one day of labor and the rent of the CO2 equipment. The owner was amazed. I wasn't. I knew my son. I was proud.

God is fitting things together for maximum effectiveness. He knows what's required to accomplish his purposes, and he knows what is inside every one of us. He understands how to team us together; how to empower each of us; how to align us top to bottom and side to side. We just need to let him be the boss.

I used to do all my oil changes. The Lord asked me one day, "How much does a mechanic charge for changing oil?"

"Twenty-seven dollars...I think."

"Well, you're worth more to me in that hour and a half it takes you to change oil."

That exchange was a paradigm shift for me. I've always been my own mechanic. In one sense, it was about changing oil. On another level, it was about time management. But in the grand scheme of things, it was a lesson on alignment. The Lord wanted me to align with people who could do this chore cheaper and faster so I could be freed up to do other things that I'm especially good at. Yet to let somebody else change my oil, I had to choose to trust them. And if you think trust was easy for this former mechanic....

In Christianity, we tend to prize zeal and passion as the highest of all affections. Yet when they're not channeled properly—when the people are not positioned and equipped—they are as ineffective as fireworks when you really need cannon fire.

Another thing about this word: "In whom you also are being built together." It means "to invent or put together words and sentences; how you form a sentence; to constitute or form as parts of the whole." Alignment is about going from A, B, C, D to run-on sentences, paragraphs and chapters. It means "to settle, to adjust, and to compose differences; to settle into a quiet state."

In Ephesians 4:16, we read:

From whom the whole body, joined and knit together by what every joint supplies, according to the effective working by which every part does its share, causes growth of the body for the edifying of itself in love.

This is an incredible scripture. It is translated from Strong's NT word #4883 *sunarmologeó*. It's root is also from Strong's #4862 *sun*. It means, "to form with suitable organs.; to construct so that one part may cooperate with the other." It also means, "to sing in parts as to organize the Hallelujah." Further, it means, "to distribute into suitable parts and appoint proper officers, that the whole may act as one body as to organize an army."

The character of an organization is comprised of the sum total of everything becoming fitly joined together. A club, a party or a faction is organized when it assumes a systemized form. Only then can it be effective at its given purpose. At this point, it can focus on conquest.

Whether it is a political team, a missionary team, a church body or a nuclear family, its purpose is going to be related to conquest.

What is conquest? Consider Romans 8:37:

But in all these things we overwhelmingly conquer through Him who loved us.

The word *conquest* is related to the words *overcomers* and *conquerors* We need the latter to do the former. It is much easier to overcome through the power of agreement, being fitly joined with others who can recognize the voice of God; who are willing and obedient. Disagreement in the ranks can be a good thing if it leads to greater understanding of purpose. However, outright dissension is a tool of the enemy to destroy alignment. This is why Paul wrote:

And being ready to punish all disobedience when your obedience is fulfilled.

2 Corinthians 10:6

To be obedient to something, we must allow others to become aligned with us; we must become aligned with them; and we must become one.

11

Faith, Favor and Providence

I SAT WITH A YOUNG APOSTLE in northwest Arkansas, and he referred to "the law of the ultimate intangible." I began to question him about it, and he said, "Well, most people would say the law of the ultimate intangible deals with favor, but it's greater than favor."

It is what David speaks of in Psalm 84:5-7.

> *Blessed is the person whose strength is in You,*
> *In whose heart are the roads to Zion!*
> *Passing through the Valley of Baca they make it a spring;*
> *The early rain also covers it with blessings.*
> *They go from strength to strength,*
> *Every one of them appears before God in Zion.*

The law of the ultimate intangible is the providence of God. To more fully understand this, let's first go to Corinthians.

> *And since we have the same spirit of faith, according to what is written, "I believed and therefore I spoke," we also believe and therefore speak.*
>
> 2 Corinthians 4:13

Now, consider two words: *ultimate* and *intangible*. When we say *ultimate*, we mean the best, the greatest, surpassing everything else we could achieve or imagine. If Susan drove up to meet me in a Lamborghini, that could be the ultimate date night car. (Although I'd prefer a new truck.)

The word *intangible* is simply something that exists but is unable to be touched or grasped except by faith; it does not have a physical presence. The blood that Jesus sprinkled on the mercy seat is real; its power is present today, but we can't see it with our eyes.

There are many things that are intangible. People say they want a better this, a better that, and I say, "I know where it is; I can tell you exactly where to find what you are seeking. It is on the inside." I am able to direct them from an intangible desire to a tangible result.

As Christians, that which is intangible has already been deposited into us. As we grow into greater communion with Holy Spirit—the intangible—he leads us to the places we should be. Sometimes, that leading comes down to a very practical direction in our lives.

I went to buy a truck that had 60,000 miles on it. Then I came down with bronchitis. I called the dealer, and I said, "I really don't need to come in. I'm sick. Can you hold it? It's a done deal. I'll take it. And I don't need any financing."

Two days later, I was feeling better. I called and said, "I'd like to come get the truck."

"Oh, the sales manager sold it," said the salesman.

Now, this particular truck was the exact model I wanted. It was the right color and had the right equipment. I was challenged.

"They sold my truck!" I said to Susan after I hung up the phone.

"There's a better one," she said calmly.

Well, I wanted to fume and sputter, but a still, small voice told me that Susan just might be on to something. (It's happened before…once or twice or ten-thousand times.) So, I began to call around, and I found the identical truck with 20,000 fewer miles and $3,000 cheaper. It was a dealer-certified used truck. That's providence!

> *For You bless the righteous person, Lord,*
> *You surround him with favor as with a shield.*
>
> Psalm 5:12

Christians talk a lot about favor—the favor of God; the favor of man. Yet we operate in something far greater than favor. Certainly, we count favors when we can buy the dress, the coat, those boots or whatever that we want, or we get the job we desired, or our daughter is admitted to medical school after enrollment is closed. That is favor.

Let's look at 2 Corinthians 4:13:

Since we have the same spirit of faith according to what is written, I believed, and therefore I spoke.

Often, we discover something in the Bible, and upon hearing it, we begin to speak it. Folks in the faith movement have been saying this for decades. And so, they should. It works!

People come to me saying: "I need you to come in agreement with me about a better job."

"What scripture are you standing on?" is my standard reply.

"Well, I don't have one."

"Then I have nothing to come in agreement with. I can't come into agreement with your whims, wishes, or hopes. How about we agree on 3 John 1:2: "Beloved, I pray that in all respects you may prosper and be in good health, just as your soul prospers."

Certainly, there is nothing wrong with whims, wishes or hopes. They are good starting points. For all we know, they may even align with God's will. However, we cannot stand on those. Standing means to withstand something, as in "having done all, to stand" (Ephesians 6:13 NKJV). Whims and wishes will position you to receive; they cannot enable you to receive. That requires grace—the power of God to obtain.

> *When we operate in the spirit of faith, it releases God's intangible providence.*

Sometimes, what we think we want is not what we really need. I had an elder's wife, a nutritionist, who took a raise and a promotion at a hospital. When she talked to me about it, I asked, "You're taking on a lot more responsibility. Is the $4,000 a year raise worth it?"

"Oh, yes. That's so much money. That's $300 a month more. I'll be able to make my car payment."

"Well, just make sure that the responsibility and the stress of the responsibility don't outweigh it."

Six months later, she came and said, "Would you pray with me that I can get my old job back? This new job is too much pressure."

God wants us to prosper in his economy, not ours. Prosperity comes in many forms. Sometimes, a job with less stress (and a lower paycheck) is prosperity. A better job could simply mean better people to work for, and better health in the long run.

When we operate in the spirit of faith, it releases God's intangible providence. However, there are several elements to it.

George Washington

During the French and Indian War, George Washington was with General Braddock fighting the French and Indian War. The Indians, were fighting with the French. The French gave the Indians rifles, and the Indians taught the French many things about warfare in the wilderness—things like how to move stealthily and how to take cover. The only way the British knew to fight was to fully expose themselves. Instead of hiding behind trees and rocks, they stood in a line in their bright red and white uniforms, fired their muskets and marched forward with bayonets fixed. Needless to say, they were being annihilated.

As one of the mounted officers, George Washington was shot at many times. In fact, four bullets went through his coat and two horses were shot out from under him. Yet nothing touched him; he escaped without a scratch. (Well, I imagine when the horse he rode in on collapsed, he might have been bruised a bit.)

Years later, he and his closest friend, Dr. Craig, were traveling through Ohio and New York, in the same area that the fighting occurred. They came upon a group of Indians. The Indian Chief said to Washington, "I know who you are. You're the great warrior that our bullets wouldn't touch."

A young warrior who was with the Chief said, "I had seven or eight great shots at you, but I couldn't touch you, because something greater than you protected you."

The Chief then asked, "Can I speak to you in the voice of prophecy? You will become a father of a great nation."

Seventeen years later, Washington became the father of our nation. Nobody can tell me we're not a Christian nation. We were started with a prophetic word.

Consider Robert Hunt. Have you ever studied who discovered America? Christopher Columbus is credited with discovering America, but few people know what Columbus wrote in his diary before he ever considered his fateful journey. He recorded an encounter with an angel who said to him, "Read the book of Job. You will discover a new world that will become light to the world."

Columbus read the Book of Job and encountered evidence that the earth was not flat, but round. Job 26:10 says: "He has inscribed a circle on the surface of the waters at the boundary of light and darkness."

In Isaiah 40:21-22, we read of the circle of the earth:

Do you not know? Have you not heard?
Has it not been declared to you from the beginning?
Have you not understood from the foundations of the earth?
It is He who sits above <u>the circle of the earth,</u>
And its inhabitants are like grasshoppers,
Who stretches out the heavens like a curtain.

George Washington Carver, famous for his work in the agronomy of peanuts, was asked by a senator, "How did you discover this about peanuts?"

"I read an old book," Carver replied.

"There's an old book that tells all this about peanuts?" asked the incredulous Senator.

"No, the old book talks about God, and He created the peanuts, and God told me the rest."

I write this to tell you today: America is a Christian nation; our destiny is in God. We have sent out more missionaries than any other nation on earth. Certainly, we deviated from God's will through grievous errors like slavery and abortion. But can I tell you: God forgives and he restores. He is not finished with us. America will be saved, and with it, the world as well.

Spirit of Faith

Let's look at how the spirit of faith works. The spirit of faith will always draw the word of faith—that word which comes from God; the word that says "You got what you asked for." The spirit of faith initiates; the word of faith consummates.

In the gospel of Matthew, we read of Jesus:

He compelled the disciples to get into the boat and to go ahead of him to the other side, while he sent the crowds away. After he had sent the crowds away, he went up on the mountain by Himself to pray; and when it was evening, he was there alone.

Matthew 14:22-23

Some hours later, deep in the night, Jesus came walking across the water and scared the life out of the disciples.

When the disciples saw Him walking on the sea, they were terrified, and said, "It is a ghost!" And they cried out in fear. But immediately Jesus spoke to them, saying, "Take courage, it is I; do not be afraid."

Matthew 14:26-27

But Peter, full of the spirit of faith, spoke up and said;

Lord, if it is You, command me to come to You on the water.

Matthew 14:28

This is what Paul meant in 2 Corinthians 4:13 when he said: "I believe and therefore I speak." Notice what happened. When Peter spoke out of the spirit of faith, the word of faith came back from Jesus.

And He [Jesus] said, "Come!"

And Peter got out of the boat and walked on the water, and came toward Jesus.

Matthew 14:29

If we're going to fulfill providence, we must allow the spirit of faith in us to speak to things bigger than us—things that require faith. Many of us are living to fulfill James 2:4: "You do not have because you do not ask." That's not a great heritage. We need to ask in the spirit of faith. You will be amazed at what comes to you through faith…in God's economy.

I sat with Freda Lindsay, the woman who led Christ for the Nations. We were in Timisoara, Romania, and one of the Bible leaders told her that the Bible school was growing and needed more room.

There was a house for sale that would do nicely. Freda asked the price; it was $37,000.

She looked at the married couple who was also traveling with us. She said, "Don't you think you need to write a check so we can buy that house right now?"

The husband looked at his wife; they had a brief discussion. He looked back at Freda and said, "We won't even have to pray about this. We're in a position to buy this house. This college needs to expand."

They wrote the check.

I came home from that trip and told Susan, "I learned a new way to take up offerings. Freda didn't manipulate that couple. She just said, "Don't you think...?"

Freda was operating in the spirit of faith, and the couple responded in the word of faith. The spirit of faith will always draw the word of faith.

Now, there will always be those who want a prophetic word before they act, and there are those who just want God to come any way that he can. The spirit of faith wants God to come anyway he can. Sometimes, people are insecure and want a prophetic word as a trophy so they can say, "John Paul Jackson prophesied to me...blah blah blah."

Well, it's great to receive a word. The determinant is what we do with it. Are we warring with it? Have we typed it out? Do we reread it and let it challenge us?

I have nearly every prophetic word ever spoken to me since I was born again. I got my first prophetic word in 1983, and I have them stored electronically. When I get alone, perhaps in a deer stand, I read every one of them. No...I *declare* every one of them. "This is what my Father said, and he doesn't lie. This is what God said, and if I will get out of his way and quit "helping" him, everything he said will come to pass."

This is providence. Psalms 84:5-7 tells us:

Blessed is the person whose strength is in You,
In whose heart are the roads to Zion!
Passing through the Valley of Baca they make it a spring;
The early rain also covers it with blessings.
They go from strength to strength,
Every one of them appears before God in Zion.

Our strength is in God. Paul says in 2 Corinthians 12:10: "When I am weak, then I am strong." The strongest words we can pray are these: "Oh God...help!"

I've been in those places. When my son-in-law, Brian, lay dying in bed, I rushed home. A group of ministers and I prayed over him; we prayed in the spirit of faith, believing for his healing. That evening, I received the word of faith, but it wasn't what I expected. The Lord told me, "Brian is not going to be healed. I'm going to receive him home."

All night, all I could do was cry out, "Oh, God!" I knew Brian was in God's hands. My heart cry was for my daughter Dawn. How could I tell her God was not going to heal her husband?

Dawn came to our home in the morning and we shared what the Lord told us. It was an emotionally difficult time. Later that day, we went to the hospital and released Brian in prayer. Seven hours later, he was in the arms of Jesus.

Faith came to us when we heard God's word, and although it wasn't what we asked for, it made the process easier. Knowing that God heard us, but that he had another plan, was of great comfort.

Blessed is the person whose strength is in You; in whose heart are the roads to Zion!

Psalm 84:5

Brian wasn't leaving us; he was entering a greater dimension of God's presence. Our lives are not static; the only constant is change.

Brian was ushered into the eternal presence of God. Indeed, God has set eternity in our hearts.

> *He has also set eternity in their heart, without the possibility that mankind will find out the work which God has done from the beginning even to the end.*
>
> Ecclesiastes 3:11

Although we don't fully grasp eternity, we do understand that eternity is our destiny. It is not a destination. Rather, it is a journey that lasts forever.

God has set eternity in the hearts of all mankind, and eternity is filled with providence.

> *Delight yourself also in the Lord,*
> *And He shall give you the desires of your heart*
> *Commit your way to the Lord,*
> *Trust also in Him,*
> *And He shall bring it to pass.*
> *He shall bring forth your righteousness as the light,*
> *And your justice as the noonday.*
>
> Psalm 37:4-6

The word *delight* means "making pliable or being contrite in the hands of God." Another word for *delight* could be the word *malleable*, meaning "able to be hammered or pressed permanently out of shape without breaking or cracking." God wants us to be bondable and malleable so he can reach into our hearts and give us our hearts' desires.

When our hearts are pliable, they are ready for a move of God. Interestingly, the Muslim world is ready. Muslims are becoming followers of Jesus by the millions. My friend Harold Eberle did a crusade in Pakistan. The people who came were a mile wide and five miles deep. Many became followers of Jesus. Months later, they were still baptizing all the new converts. It's not easy to minister there, however. When he preaches in Pakistan, a guy with a shotgun stands on one side of him, a guy with a pistol is on his other side, and a guy with a rifle is perched on the roof above him. But it's worth it; people are becoming followers of Jesus.

Years ago, the Lord told me, "There will be a move of God among the Muslims that will provoke the Jews to jealousy." I've met some incredible people who are of the Muslim faith; they simply need Jesus. Amen? They just need to know Jesus.

God is making all of our hearts pliable: believers and non-believers. We will not fully discover our destiny until we come to that place where we are contrite. God does this in unusual ways.

My Experience

When I look back on my life, I often wonder, "Why Lord? Why did I live?" I wasn't raised in church; I was raised a heathen. I lived a bad life. I hurt people for pleasure. I was a fighter; I hurt a lot of people. I've been stabbed. Six men beat me one time and left me for dead. I was six weeks in the hospital.

Why did I live through all that? Why did I live through the drug craze when I was abusing prescription drugs and drinking alcohol, driving 5,000 miles a week in a tractor-trailer? Why did I wake up many nights with my eighteen-wheeler in the median, running eighty miles an hour, and never have an accident? Why did I live through all that?

Why?

I believe it was providence. Eternity is in our hearts. God put it there. We can't escape it. After I beat a man to a pulp, I'd walk away with my heart hurting because I hurt him. The anger fueled me to do wrong, but my heart was bent towards God. There was a sensitivity, a pliability to my nature even though I had not been born again. That tenderness allowed the providence to work. He set eternity within me when he formed in my mother's womb.

Aligned for Conquest

As a five-year-old boy, struck down with encephalitis (brain swelling), I laid seven months paralyzed in a hospital bed. Doctors said I'd never live, yet God in his providence knew that day would come. He placed someone in my life—our housekeeper who knew God and prophesied to my unbelieving parents, "Don't worry. God done told me he's going to heal Clay, and he's going to preach the gospel all over the world."

As of this writing, I've been to fifty-nine nations of the world and counting. This is not about me. It's about God's intangible providence.

I wrote about this earlier but it bears repeating. In 1931, my grandfather hired a black man who was near starvation. Robert became the best employee my grandfather had; they formed a lifelong bond. In 1958, my dad and his crew were working under a car when a hot work light fell off a bench into a bucket of gasoline and exploded. Every white man in the shop ran out and left my dad to burn.

But see, God knew in 1931 that this day was coming. Robert Caperton dragged my dad outside and extinguished the flames. Dad was carried to Cambell's clinic and he laid there for nine months. They took skin off his body and grafted it to his arm. They told my mother two or three times that gangrene had set in and they might have to amputate his arm. They weren't praying, but somehow, they knew that God was working. When Dad finally healed, you couldn't see a scar on him; incredible, considering how badly he was burned. There was providence in his life.

Winston Churchill's life was saved twice by the same man—the son of the gardener. Young Churchill was swimming in the family's pond and began struggling. The gardener's son jumped in and saved him. When Winston's dad came home, he thanked the son. He told the gardener: "If I can ever be a blessing to your son, I will."

The gardener said, "My son wants to go to higher learning."

Faith, Favor and Providence

In England at that time, you only got into higher learning if you were upper class. When the time came, Mr. Churchill helped the gardener's son go to college. The son became a medical doctor.

Years later, Winston Churchill was in Egypt and became so sick that he was not expected to live. Then a young doctor said: "I think I just discovered something that will heal him." They flew him to Egypt and treated him with the new drug. The doctor was the gardener's son, Alexander Fleming, and he had discovered penicillin.

These things were not a coincidence. These occurrences could have gone wrong in many ways. What if Mr. Churchill had not fulfilled his promise to bless the gardener's son? What if my grandfather would've been a racist and told that starving black man to go away? This was during the great depression. Robert Caperton went to work for my grandfather in 1931 and worked for the Nash family until 1978. Robert became a Nash and a relative of mine. He was family.

These are examples of God's providence. The question before us is this: do we want providence to work at a higher level? God's providence is going to work on our behalf at a greater level than it ever has. But we must come to a place where our hearts are even more surrendered to God.

> *And we know that God causes all things to work together for good to those who love God, to those who are called according to His purpose. For those whom He foreknew, He also predestined to become conformed to the image of His Son, so that He would be the firstborn among many brothers and sisters; and these whom He predestined, He also called; and these whom He called, He also justified; and these whom He justified, He also glorified.*
>
> Romans 8:28-30 (NASB)

There's providence in our lives—it is the life of Jesus Christ. If you can get this, you can go to another level. If you catch it, you're going to go to the place where you know God as Jehovah-Jireh.

Aligned for Conquest

Grace and peace be multiplied to you in the knowledge of God, and of Jesus our Lord, as His divine power has given to us all things that pertain to life and godliness.

2 Peter 1:2-3

This understanding comes straight from heaven, but its roots reach deep into the practical aspect of our lives. Worry can kill; it's a close cousin to fear. If we are worried about a washing machine breaking down, that's not life in godliness. If we're worried about our car, the taxes, the tires…it erodes our faith and tarnishes our witness. I preached all over the South in the '80s, driving on Maypop tires. Do you know that brand? They may pop at any moment. Yet God's providence was upon us.

We preached a revival in Gideon, Missouri. It took everything that came in with the offering, $376, to pay for our bills, food and fuel. We slept in the church. Our kids thought we were camping out. I wasn't quite as excited about it as they were. But we did that, and we drove home on the cheapest set of tires I could get at Walmart for $243. We drove home, and a man who had been in those services wrote me to say: "I just wish I could hear God like you. I've never seen anybody recognize the voice of God like you. I just want to plant this seed into your life, and I want you to ask you to pray for me to hear God."

The amount he sent was $243. God knew we needed the tires, and he knew how much we needed to get them.

Another time, we were headed home for Christmas in our hometown. We spent the night at Susan's parents' house. That night, I had a dream about an ad in the newspaper called The Arkansas Democrat. In the dream, it said: "Volkswagen Jetta diesel, $1,000."

I told Susan, "I had this dream last night, that we needed a second vehicle and it was a thousand dollars."

I looked in the classified and there it was, Volkswagen Jetta diesel, $1000. I called the lady and I said, "I need to buy your car; tell me about it. Can I meet you and check it out?"

I checked it out and liked it. So, I asked, "Is there any way you can hold the title long enough to let me get back home and get the money?"

She said, "No, I got to have the money now."

So, I called my banker. I had just sold an old pickup truck and had the cash at home. I told him, "I've got $1,600 at home. Is there any way you would wire $1,000 and I'll come in and pay you for the wire and everything when I get back after Thanksgiving?"

He said, "I've never done this before, and every time I've ever helped a preacher, it's been a very bad story. But I will help you, Clay."

He wired the money. We drove the Volkswagen home. We pulled it in the driveway, got the mail, and there was a letter from the same man who bought the tires. "I Just had you on my heart," he said. "I sold a few cows and got more for them than I expected. I just wanted to give you a thousand dollars."

Providence. The providence of God is realized through the measure of faith that God gives each of us.

Romans 12:3 says:

For through the grace given to me I say to everyone among you not to think more highly of himself than he ought to think; but to think so as to have sound judgment, as God has allotted to each a measure of faith.

Within each of us is the need for providence to work. Looking back over my life, I've watched the providence of God grow. It works. It worked when I didn't have faith. It worked when I didn't have enough faith. It worked for the man who cried out to Jesus on behalf of his demon-possessed son: "I do believe; help my unbelief!" (Mark 9:24).

Providence will work even with a little bit of faith. It's the law of the ultimate intangible. It's inside every one of us. When you tap into this, on the level that God wants you to tap into it, then the reality of Isaiah 8:18 manifests:

> *Here am I and the children whom the Lord has given me!*
> *We are for signs and wonders in Israel*
> *From the Lord of hosts,*
> *Who dwells in Mount Zion.*

In my heathen days, I ran hard with the devil. You can read about it in Jim Bryson's book about my life: *The Real Deal.* Today, many people who knew me back then have reconnected with me on social media and are watching the life I now live in Christ. They make statements like: "You live the life we all want to live."

My answer is simple: I live the life God has prepared for me, and he has prepared the same life for you. You can live it too…if you accept it.

Sometimes, I hear: "I wish I had your faith. I wish I was a preacher so I could be blessed like you."

I tell them: "God doesn't bless me because I'm a preacher. He blesses me because I'm a son of God. You can be a son (daughter) of God as well! Here's how…"

I finished preaching one evening and a woman I know from childhood, Elane Wentworth, approached me. We went to elementary and junior high school together until I got kicked out of school. However, we kept the friendship. I worked with her dad and her uncle for many years. Later, her uncle worked for me in my fabrication shop. Elane's grandchild had been recently born with medical complications and was back in the hospital. Elane's request was a common one: "I know God listens to your prayers."

That gave me the opportunity to say, "He listens to your prayers, too. It's the power of agreement that you are seeking. You pray and I pray and the power of agreement of our prayers moves more than either prayer by itself."

> *Are you ready to go to the next level?*
> *Stir up the spirit of faith that is within you.*

I sat with a farmer in Mississippi, down in the delta region where blues singers such as Muddy Waters and Robert Johnson came from. This farmer discovered something profound—the land must respond to his voice and his faith. He told me, "I don't go and tell it to make a certain number of bushels to the acre. I command the land to give up the nutrients that the seeds need to make a better crop."

He's running twenty to twenty-five bushels an acre more than anybody else. He's having corn ears that are way bigger than anybody else's.

There is a principle at work here. When God met Moses in Exodus 3:5, he told him:

Do not come near here; remove your sandals from your feet, for the place on which you are standing is holy ground.

God was actually speaking of a principle that Moses had yet to learn. He was saying to Moses: "You're a holy man, and that ground must respond to you."

There's another level of living that is available to each and every one of us. When Jesus looked down from the cross and said "It is finished," providence was given to all mankind.

Are you ready to go to the next level?

Stir up the spirit of faith that is within you. I love when there's a spirit of faith on someone. It draws me to them. God has to work with you right where you are. You don't have to be perfect for him to work with you. That's impossible anyway. God doesn't require perfection; he requires surrender. Many people know how to be obedient to the things of God, but their hearts are not always in surrender to God. He's

Aligned for Conquest

not looking for us to be perfect; he's looking for us to be *perfected*, matured, fitly joined together, aligned into one new man.

Conclusion

The Ultimate Alignment

THE TITLE, *Aligned for Conquest,* tells us many things.

First, that we *can* be aligned.

Second, that we *should* be aligned.

Third, *why* we are to be aligned.

Alignment, in and of itself, is neutral. It is a deal brokered through relationship, sealed with a common understanding, a commitment, a vow. It enables the power of agreement, which itself is also neutral. The builders of the Tower of Babel knew the power of agreement. They were aligned. They just didn't know the providence of Holy God.

Fundamentally, alignment is the joining of lives: one life to another in strength and weakness, in good and bad, supply and need, fear and courage; nothing held back; nothing hidden. All is shared in the union of body, soul and spirit. This is what the early church experienced.

> *And the congregation of those who believed were of one heart and soul; and not one of them claimed that anything belonging to him was his own, but all things were common property to them.*
>
> Acts 4:32

Of course, we align on different levels for varying purposes. We align in prayer; align in ministry; align in business; align in friendship. Marriage is the ultimate alignment. It is the full joining of every aspect of our life with another's life. Profound and irrevocable—ask anyone who has experienced the utter devastation of divorce—it is the union of all we have and all we are; the two becoming one; sharing all things equally.

> *For this reason a man shall leave his father and his mother and be joined to his wife, and the two shall become one flesh. This mystery is great; but I am speaking with reference to Christ and the church.*
>
> 1 Corinthians 7:31

It was to this bond of marriage that God sent his son to save a woefully lost humanity and reconcile us to himself. Jesus' death on the cross was not to suffer in man's place but to join himself to man through the alignment of a blood covenant—a marriage. Through this alignment, man now shared in everything Jesus had, and Jesus shared in everything man had. Jesus had the wealth of heaven through relationship with the Father. Man had the earth…and sin. Through alignment, our sins became Jesus' sins, and his righteousness became our righteousness. Our sins were dealt with through alignment, and our new life was realized through his resurrection.

To be in Christ is to be aligned with the Father through Christ. When we align as men and women of God, we are tapping into the power of agreement that was released the moment Jesus cried out: "Father, forgive them!" His profound utterance: "It is finished," declared the formation of an alignment that would sustain mankind through countless generations. All had been reconciled; all had been forgiven; all had been restored.

Therefore, when we align with one another—when we share the power of agreement through relational alignment—we stand in the blood covenant that the Father established to reconcile mankind to himself. It is through this relationship—and all relationships modeled after it—that the Father bestows upon his children all we can ask or imagine. When we operate in alignment, we stand upon the altar which lies at the foundation of the world.

Alignment requires sacrifice; it requires the laying down of our individual rights for the benefit of mutual rights. Alignment is at the heart of all life. It is who we are in Christ. Nothing can withstand those who are aligned with God.

> *What then shall we say to these things? If God is for us, who is against us? He who did not spare His own Son, but delivered Him over for us all, how will He not also with Him freely give us all things? Who will bring charges against God's elect? God is the one who justifies; who is the one who condemns? Christ Jesus is He who died, but rather, was raised, who is at the right hand of God, who also intercedes for us. Who will separate us from the love of Christ? Will tribulation, or trouble, or persecution, or famine, or nakedness, or danger, or sword? Just as it is written:*
>
> *"For Your sake we are killed all day long;*
> *We were regarded as sheep to be slaughtered."*
>
> *But in all these things we overwhelmingly conquer through Him who loved us. For I am convinced that neither death, nor life, nor angels, nor principalities, nor things present, nor things to come, nor powers, nor height, nor depth, nor any other created thing will be able to separate us from the love of God that is in Christ Jesus our Lord.*
>
> Romans 8:31-39

Let us align, go forth and conquer!

Made in the USA
Monee, IL
15 November 2024